Date Due

CONTRIBUTORS

LOUIS BALTHAZAR
A member and former head of the Department of Political Science, Laval University, Quebec City. He is a specialist in international relations and Canadian politics and is co-editor of *International Perspectives*, published by the Department of External Affairs.

MICHAEL BLISS
Professor of History at the University of Toronto. To date his major work has been in the field of Canadian business history. He is the author of the recent prize-winning biography *A Canadian Millionaire: The Life and Times of Sir Joseph Flavelle, Bart., 1858-1939.*

ROBERT CRAIG BROWN
Professor of History at the University of Toronto and past president of the Canadian Historical Association. He has written widely on post-Confederation Canadian political history and is the author of the first major study of Robert L. Borden.

R. KENNETH CARTY
A member of the Department of Political Science, University of British Columbia, he is a specialist in European and Canadian politics.

RAMSAY COOK
Professor of History at York University, Toronto. A distinguished student of French Canada, he is well known for *Canada and the French-Canadian Question* and *The Maple Leaf Forever: Essays on Nationalism and Politics in Canada*. His writings on a broad range of themes in modern Canadian history appear frequently.

J.R. MALLORY
R.B. Angus Professor of Political Science, McGill University. He has written widely on important constitutional and governmental questions and is perhaps best known for *The Structure of Canadian Government.*

H.V. NELLES
Associate Professor of History at York University, Toronto, he is the author of *The Politics of Development*, a major study of the state and natural-resource development in Ontario from 1850 to 1940.

DONALD SMILEY
Professor of Political Science at York University, Toronto. One of Canada's leading students of Canadian federalism, he is a former president of the Canadian Political Science Association and is the author of *Canada in Question: Federalism in the Eighties.*

DENIS SMITH
Professor of Political Studies, Trent University. Well known for his provocative writings on Canadian politics and politicians, he is the author of a recent biography of Walter Gordon and has just completed a term as editor of *The Canadian Forum.*

W. PETER WARD
Teaches history at the University of British Columbia. He is the author of *White Canada Forever*, a study of Asian-White relations in British Columbia.

ENTERING THE EIGHTIES
Canada in Crisis

Edited by
R. Kenneth Carty
W. Peter Ward

16113709

Toronto
Oxford University Press
1980

Canadian Cataloguing in Publication Data

Main entry under title:
Entering the eighties

ISBN 0-19-540364-9

1. Federal government — Canada — Addresses, essays,
lectures.   2. Canada — Politics and government —
Addresses, essays, lectures.   I. Carty, R. Kenneth,
1944-   II. Ward, William Peter, 1943-

JL65 1980.E57   320.971   C80-094821-1

©Oxford University Press Canada 1980
ISBN 0-19-540364-9
1 2 3 4 — 3 2 1 0
Printed in Canada by
Webcom Limited

CONTENTS

PREFACE

These essays were written for a noon-hour lecture series entitled 'Canada at Midlife Crisis', held at the University of British Columbia in February and March 1980. A program of lectures on major Canadian public issues, it was sponsored jointly by the Departments of History and Political Science, using special funds provided by the Faculty of Arts. Four distinguished scholars from each of the two disciplines were invited by the departments to deliver an address in the series. The topics discussed were not of the authors' choosing but rather were selected by the program's organizers with a view to stimulating informed discussion within the university community. While the lecture subjects were chosen for their timely nature, the full extent of their currency became apparent only as the series proceeded. Events have a way of overtaking existing plans, as they indeed did in this case.

The series was arranged in the summer of 1979, shortly after the Conservative government led by Joe Clark came into power. The recently defeated Liberal Party was in disarray, and the future of its leadership was clouded by doubt. The Clark administration seemed reasonably secure in its prospects, at least for the time being. The two major problems confronting it were the coming referendum on sovereignty-association and the growing discrepancy between domestic and world prices on petroleum products.

At the time these essays were being drafted, in the final months of 1979, it was generally assumed that the next major event on the nation's political agenda would be the long-awaited referendum. Though the date was still unannounced, it was expected to be in the not-too-distant future. In Quebec, the Parti Québécois seemed very much in command of events. The Clark administration had no significant support there and the federal Liberals from Quebec seemed powerless in defeat. Opponents of sovereignity-association clearly had no alternative to the *status quo,* and Claude Ryan had only begun to weld the scattered forces of opposition into an effective coalition. His 'beige paper' was still a thing of the future.

At the same time the inter-regional conflict over energy pricing, with its heavy overtones of western alienation, appeared increasingly likely to be resolved, despite the continued escalation of world energy prices and the pronounced shift of financial capital from one region of Canada to another. The Conservative government seemed to be working towards an agreement with Alberta, the leading advocate of provincial supremacy over resource policy and revenues.

The sudden fall of the Clark government in December 1979, and the subsequent defeat of the Conservatives at the polls the following February, substantially altered the complexion of the political scene at the mid-point of the lecture series. (Professors Balthazar and Smith, for example, each refer to different prime ministers who were in office when their respective lectures were delivered.) First, and most important of all, these events introduced a new and dramatic development in the referendum issue, one that had the power to alter substantially the terms of the referendum debate and the way it would be conducted. To be more specific, they returned to power the most implacable and articulate foe of sovereignty-association, Pierre Elliott Trudeau, and restored French Canadians to a position of major influence in federal politics. Second, they confirmed the inability of the federal political parties to win support from both founding cultures and all major regions of the country. And third, they revived the bitter feud between Ottawa and Edmonton over the price of oil and natural gas. As Professor Brown perceptively observes, one should never discount the interplay of character and circumstance in the shaping of human affairs.

Thus these essays were written and delivered in turbulent political times. The six months of Conservative government proved but a brief interregnum. The march of French-English tensions seemed to be inexorably driving the nation towards the brink of crisis. And the dispute over energy policy, with its profound implications for the national distribution of wealth, was far from a resolution.

In the months since the end of the lecture series a measure of calm has prevailed. The defeat of the Parti Québécois's request for a mandate to negotiate sovereignty-association (however ambiguous the outcome of the referendum was) has temporarily resolved one of the major questions in French-English relations. Quebec sovereignty will not likely be at issue in any constitutional talks held in the near future. Meanwhile negotiations are underway to find a petroleum pricing formula that will be agreeable to both Ottawa and Alberta. At the moment the two parties seem to be at loggerheads and open conflict might erupt at any time. In Ottawa a majority government is back in office and prospects of major changes in the federal administration now seem rather remote.

But while these essays were written in unsettled times and were addressed mainly to current issues, they also transcend the immediate concerns of the present. Their authors offer all of us compelling insights as we confront these questions on the threshold of the eighties.

We would like to thank the Dean of Arts, R.M. Will, our department heads, Alan C. Cairns and R.V. Kubicek, and colleagues too numerous to mention for the encouragement and assistance so freely offered during the lecture series and the preparation of this book.

RKC
WPW
Vancouver
21 May 1980

R. Kenneth Carty
W. Peter Ward

INTRODUCTION

Who are we?
What are we doing together?
How shall we go about our common business?

For over two hundred years Canadians and *Canadiens* have asked themselves these questions. It may be no exaggeration to suggest that the essence of the Canadian experience can be found in an endless debate over these very questions. There has been no single vision of Canada to which the nation could subscribe, and we have placed little faith in those who claimed to offer one. Rather, like Job, Canadians have sat on their rocky bit of ground, perplexed by their existence and uncertain of its meaning. But they have also determined to endure.

Canadians have never reached a consensus on the first two of these questions. In the absence of one, the institutions that have ordered our common business have inevitably proved vulnerable and fragile. We have experimented with several constitutional forms over the last two centuries. The most recent, the Confederation agreement, has been lasting and successful—so successful that many Canadians now count its age against it. But as we enter the 1980s it is clear that, because of continuing disagreement over our identity and common purpose, we must once more seek a new constitution. In the words of Denis Smith, 'the Canadian federation lies prostrate and disarmed, the purpose and determination of 1867 drained away.'

As Canadians seek to reconstitute their political arrangements, it is evident that a national consensus is no more possible, or indeed desirable, now than it has been in the past. Rather than seeking one, we should acknowledge the ambiguous sense of community that colours our history. This, as much as our hopes for the future, must shape the new constitutional arrangements we seek to make for ourselves. In the debates that lie ahead, our political leaders will operate from unstated, and often apparently contradictory, assumptions about the answers to these questions. Many Canadians will no doubt find the confusion that will result frustrating. But this too is a national tradition, one that we should have no cause to regret, for in the past it has paradoxically served Canadians quite well.

Given this situation, the pessimist might question the value of further discussion. After all, what good is served by constant inconclusive debate? One can only reply that such matters as the identity, purpose, and functioning of a nation are the great issues of modern society, and each community and each age must resolve them anew. That task has fallen to Canadians at the dawn of the 1980s, and to the ongoing deliberations all the writers in this volume have made a contribution. While never presuming to give definitive answers, they have clarified the fundamental problems of community in Canada. What is (but should not be) surprising is that there are still new things to say about these perennial questions that continue to haunt us.

Who are we?

Until very recently, most English-speaking Canadians thought of themselves as British. Recall Sir John A. Macdonald's evocative cry in 1891, 'A British subject I was born—a British subject I will die.' A sense of being British, of being part of the Empire—the greatest political creation of its time—was central to the identity of Anglo-Canadian society, as Professors Smiley and Smith both remind us. This was all too familiar to French Canadians, for it was in the hothouse climate of imperialist nationalism that they struggled to nurture their own nationalist aspirations. For them the central fact was the Conquest. It set the fundamental terms and patterns of political accommodation between the French and British in British North America: in particular it led to the subordination of the former to the latter.

Ramsay Cook traces the psychological consequences of this condition for French Canadians. He writes: 'Fear of the future and hope for the future combine to create indecision, ambiguity, paradox.' Driven by an ongoing struggle for cultural survival, French Canada has sought a definition of the nation as a bicultural partnership. As Cook points out, this has led French Canadians to adopt two alternate strategies for dealing with English Canada: one-party politics and provincial autonomy, which he labels 'French power' and 'fortress Quebec'. The reason the Confederation agreement has endured for more than a century is because it created a framework within which French Canadians could pursue both of these strategies. Twenty-five years ago Pierre Elliott Trudeau argued that federalism was the ideal system for the French in Canada. Other systems, offering fewer means for dealing with the English, might have led to one of their assimilationist nightmares. Nevertheless federalism has exacted its price, for it has required that French Canadians speak with at least two voices. Today Mr Lévesque and Mr Trudeau both represent Quebec, but they are opponents, and their antagonism reflects the ambivalence that has marked French Canada since the Conquest.

If federalism has given French Canadians an accommodation mechanism that assisted their survival, they—or the nationalists among them—have been constantly reminded of their subordinate position in North America. With the growing conviction that a people can be whole only when they possess full political sovereignty has come a demand for national self-determination in Quebec. Donald Smiley's essay discusses this development and emphasizes the importance of government's role in linking ethnicity and political organization. Pursuing this theme further, Louis Balthazar argues that it was the *politically* directed modernization of the province, led by an aggressive and newly confident provincial government, that transformed French Canada and French Canadians. Central to this process has been a political metamorphosis: 'French Canadians have become Québécois.' This, as Balthazar implies, was surely the most important consequence of the Quiet Revolution. With a new name, French Canadians have declared themselves a new people, and so they seek a new accommodation with English Canada. The Parti Québécois represents a dimension of the French Canadian psyche that, in Ramsay Cook's terms, longs for freedom; their political manifesto calls upon the Québécois to make a dash for it.

However, like Cook, Balthazar knows that this interpretation distorts the essence of modern Quebec. French Canada cannot escape its past, with all its ambiguities, and so the referendum proposal, which called upon the people of Quebec to decide in favour of or against Canada, posed a false dichotomy. The reality is that the majority of Québécois are in the process of defining themselves as citizens. Their growing self-awareness will inevitably challenge and threaten the French who live outside Quebec. It will also stimulate changes in the way English Canadians see themselves. The results of all these self-examinations will profoundly affect the political compromises that will undoubtedly shape any future revisions of the political order.

If French Canada has undergone a process of redefinition, so has the rest of the country—though with much less sense of purpose. Indeed, as Smiley points out, the failure of English-speaking Canada as a whole to embrace the notion of cultural duality stems not so much from its insensitivity to the transformation of Quebec as from an awareness that it is culturally heterogeneous. The transformation of the rest of the country from a British society to a multicultural one is difficult for Québécois separatists to accept, for it runs against their political catechism, but the cultural pluralism of English-speaking Canada is now one of the undeniable aspects of our identity. While Mr Clark can call Canada a community of communities, federalist politicians from Quebec, like Mr Trudeau, appear to be genuinely perplexed by the idea. In fact the complexity of the Canadian mosaic leads Smiley to suggest that we return to the notion (which, with Canadian irony, can be traced to George-Etienne Cartier) that Canadians should seek a limited *political nationality.*

If this seems a vague, liberal, and rather modest way of thinking about the answer to the question Who are we?, Canadians need not be discouraged, for we are a modest people at heart. Our great political achievement has been to create a system that, in spite of differing regional and cultural interests, permits us to live together in freedom, tolerance, and decency.

The essays in this volume (and the inclinations of our politicians) leave little doubt that some form of 'renewed federalism' is likely. The dynamic forces that have made our old self-definitions less and less relevant now require that we seek new patterns for our political lives. Canadian politicians have been on this quest for over a decade and the outcome of the referendum in Quebec may yet provide the strongest incentive to achieve creative and workable revisions in our political system.

What are we doing together?
Though Macdonald intended to die a British subject, he busied himself with building a Canadian state. Since Cartier's political community was more a declaration of faith than a statement of reality—after all, eighteen of the nineteen Nova Scotians elected to the first Parliament in 1867 had run on a separatist platform—early Canadian governments were determined that the state would build the nation. There is nothing peculiarly Canadian about the activist state. As Smiley says, it is a widespread phenomenon in the modern world. What is of interest here is the Canadian variation on this theme.

In most modern communities the role and activity of the state are the subject of dusty academic tomes and vigorous partisan conflict. In Canada the activist role of the state has produced a public myth: that government intervention has had a positive effect on the shaping of the nation. Even though it is clear that the national government has not always acted in our best economic interests, we still seem to think that it has bound the nation together. Thus, despite being divided by obvious regional, linguistic, economic, social, religious, and legal differences, Canada has long been assumed to be an integrated community because of the achievements and activities of the central government.

Michael Bliss attacks this article of national faith head on by reviewing the effects of the National Policy, that icon of Canadian nationalists, and the impact of public-sector entrepreneurialism in the twentieth century. His conclusions parallel those of the nineteenth-century liberals who opposed such policies: Canadians are poorer for the state's activities as 'manager, regulator, and entrepreneur'. However, Bliss argues that a widespread acceptance of this view would not 'have any particular impact on the real world of policy formation'. For those who think public policy should be based on reason, this assumption might seem rather discouraging. But we should remind ourselves that in developing federal policies—for example, in building national transportation and broadcasting systems—government activity has helped to create a national consciousness. In effect it has laid the foundations for a national mythology. There is another side to this achievement, however: national myths constitute an enormous political resource for any politicians who can harness them. They invite exploitation, and in the twentieth century the Liberals have come to learn this lesson best. It is no coincidence that they displaced the Conservatives, who had been Canada's government party until the turn of the century.

Today opposition to government activity is considered to be almost unCanadian. Reliance on feed from the public trough has now spread well beyond big business, which had fattened there for so long. Our appetite for subsidies verges on gluttony. But both Smiley and Bliss warn that this growing dependence on governmental assistance threatens the basic liberties that Canadians value. Although far removed from the world of government grants, recent investigations into the activities of the Royal Canadian Mounted Police have shown what right- and left-wing critics have long argued: the state is not neutral and will go to great lengths to protect what it defines as appropriate behaviour, including what it considers to be acceptable political ideas.

Interventionist government, so central to national mythology, is no longer characteristic of Ottawa alone. The last two decades have seen the rapid growth of provincial government activity, much of it defended in the context of building and sustaining distinctive provincial communities. While this activity has perhaps been most evident in Quebec in the wake of the Quiet Revolution, it has also gained momentum in the West, where resource riches are adding clout to the latest round of protests against the interests of the centre.

Energy policy constitutes a particularly appropriate symbol of these changes, for it brings the conflicting interests of the western provinces and Ottawa clearly into focus. Our political nationalism suggests that there ought to be a national energy policy, and that we need national instruments (i.e., those of the central government) to administer it. But the western provinces, especially Alberta, argue that any such policy would inevitably operate against *their* interests and so must be opposed. The recent national election confirmed the views of federal politicians, while successive Alberta elections have given Mr Lougheed a mandate to develop an Alberta-first policy. Here we see how the tradition of activist government has provoked intractable federal-provincial conflict—so much so that inter-governmental conferences now make compelling daytime television.

In an effort to confront this issue, H.V. Nelles takes a critical look at Canadian energy policy in the years since the Second World War. His conclusion is stark: for both constitutional and practical reasons, a national energy policy is not possible. Nelles's not unreasonable conclusion is that we should accept this fact and pursue policy strategies accordingly. Doubtless his advice will not make popular reading east of Winnipeg. (It was received with considerable applause in Vancouver, and one shudders to think of its reception in Edmonton.) But it raises questions that should not be ignored. Will Canadians, and in particular the national government, abandon the idea of national energy policy, as Nelles suggests they should? Probably not, for if they did, their deepest beliefs about the role of the Canadian state would be challenged, and their traditional understanding of the Canadian political community undermined.

How shall we go about our common business?
Perhaps because of the fascination with the intricacies of federalism and the complexities of the British North America Act, we have paid remarkably little attention to other aspects of our political life. So uninformed are we that when the Liberals were defeated at the polls in the spring of 1979, it seemed to come as a major surprise to many Canadians, including the national-affairs reporters for CBC television, that in the aftermath of an inconclusive election a Prime Minister could actually wait to meet Parliament and would be acting quite properly if he did so. If this is an indictment of civic education and educators, as well as political scientists, it also suggests that there is much more to our political life than its federal character.

Long before Canadians believed in democracy as it is expressed by universal sufferage, or in federalism, they were convinced of the virtues of parliamentary responsible government. There have never been serious proposals for constitutional reform that advocated moving away from our parliamentary system of government. Opposition to any reform of the Senate that would enhance its role is often based firmly on the conviction that such a change would necessarily undermine the established principles of responsible government. Nevertheless parliaments do change—not quickly, nor in response to the whims of public opinion, but largely to suit the needs of their members and the interests they represent. In his discussion of the parliamentary reforms we can expect in the 1980s, Professor Mallory emphasizes the continuity and coherence that parliamentary tradition brings to our public life. Of the changes he foresees, the introduction of proportional representation to the electoral system would be the most dramatic and most obvious. This could well lead to coalition government as a normal feature of the system, which would be a significant departure from the adversarial traditions we have developed. Such changes raise many questions. For instance, would they spill over into provincial arenas? Would they affect federal-provincial relations? Would they lead to more responsive patterns of public policy or to stalemate? There are no answers to these questions because these are not matters that can be legislated. New forms of parliamentary practice would evolve gradually as traditions became modified under the pressure of new circumstances. How this might happen would depend on the individuals returned to Parliament and what they chose to make of their opportunities. Mallory warns us that, if we are to exploit our parliamentary tradition to the fullest advantage, we shall have to think carefully about the kind of people we elect.

According to Denis Smith, however, if the recent past is any guide, prospects for creative Canadian politics are rather bleak, at least in the short term. His survey of the conduct of the major parties during our current constitutional and political malaise has left him pessimistic. He provides a convincing case for believing that the federal parties 'have abdicated any serious role in the constitutional debate' and suggests that only in Quebec are there political parties that, as parties, have anything to say about the fundamental questions facing the country. This suggests that more than ever Canadians will effectively be denied any opportunity of significantly influencing the reshaping of their country. It is all rather reminiscent of the events that led to Confederation in 1867, when democratic considerations were much less significant. Then politicians reorganized the political map of British North America in a series of closed-door conferences. They did so primarily to suit their purposes, and with some opposition from the public. Will their political heirs do the same, this time as the defenders of vast governmental interests? Canadians concerned with prospects for a renewed Canada, and for the organization and distribution of power within it, might well ponder Smith's observations.

Whatever the state of our parties, it is our political leaders who will sit down together to work out our new constitutional arrangements. The skills, temperaments, and frailties they bring to the conference table will doubtless have a substantial (and largely unpredictable) influence on the results of their deliberations. Craig Brown's impressionistic survey of Canadian political leaders emphasizes, time and again, that personality is crucial in political decision-making. The ways in which Canada's Prime Ministers have responded to circumstances—have seized opportunities or have been driven by events—prove the folly of any quest for simple laws in human affairs, past or present. And lest we think our leaders are in full command of all they survey, Brown reminds us that the gods of fortune cannot be denied: they may dump their chamber pots upon our unsuspecting heads. Surely in the result of the Quebec referendum, with all its ambiguity, we can see the workings of Fortune. As we enter the eighties it matters greatly how our political leaders meet the events that confront them. The outcome of these encounters will bear heavily on the future of our country and ultimately on our very sense of what it is to be Canadian.

I
Nation and Nationality

Donald Smiley

REFLECTIONS ON CULTURAL NATIONHOOD AND POLITICAL COMMUNITY IN CANADA

The demand of self-determination is the claim that a group that defines itself as a people should not be governed by those whom its members regard as foreigners, or share the powers of government with foreigners. It must be emphasized that self-determination is a matter of self-definition rather than of such objective group characteristics as race, culture, language, and religion. Contrary to the expectation of sophisticated social scientists as recently as two decades ago, the continuing processes of modernization with their consequent homogenization of values, life styles, and so on have in many parts of the developed world been accompanied by the heightened assertion of cultural and other particularisms and by strains on what were regarded as the stablest of political communities.[1] For example, the modernization of Quebec has resulted both in the weakening of the religious and cultural differences that in the past most clearly distinguished that society from its English-speaking environment, *and* in the rise of Québécois nationalism.[2] Further, the independence movement draws its leadership and the stablest elements of its electoral support from those groups of Québécois who are more like other Canadians than are their compatriots. And, significantly, the spokesmen of the contemporary independence movement, unlike Quebec nationalists in the past, are not disposed to emphasize English-French differences other than language.

Self-determination in its modern form is the assertion of the rights of peoples as defined by culture, ethnicity, religion, and language, or a combination of these. Self-determination is thus *national* self-determination, a demand that the boundaries of state and nation be made to coincide.

As is well known, the principle of national self-determination stems from the period of the French Revolution.[3] Despite the universalistic appeals of that Revolution to the rights of man and of nations, what was here successfully affirmed was the rights of the *French* nation; the leaders of France in their subsequent adventures appealed to other culturally defined peoples in Europe to rise up against *their* rulers in asserting the principle of nationality. But, once asserted, the principle could not be contained, and the defeat of Napoleonic France was in large part a result of the resistance of other Europeans to being ruled by Frenchmen.

It might be mentioned that the other revolution of the late eighteenth century—that of the United States—was much less destabilizing in its consequences for political order, because the Americans defined themselves as a people in exclusively political rather than cultural, linguistic, ethnic, or religious terms. Here is John Jay in the Second Federalist Paper: 'Providence has been pleased to give this one connected country to one united people—a people descended from the same ancestors, speaking the same language, professing the same religion, attached to the same principles of government, very similar in their manners and customs, and who, by their joint counsels, arms, and efforts, fighting side by side through a long and bloody war, have established general liberty and independence.' In Jay's view, then, the non-political bonds of the community had been given by Providence and the political bonds had been forged by the political acts of fighting a war for independence and establishing new forms of political allegiance and political organization. It is true of course that what constituted a people *did* become problematic for Americans of the next century. The Civil War was essentially a conflict about whether 'We, the people of the United States' meant that the people had constituted themselves once and for all into an indissoluble union or whether 'We, the people' referred to individuals as citizens of their respective states who through such states retained the continuing right to withdraw from the union as they chose. But popular sovereignty in its American context has related to political and constitutional organization alone rather than to such non-political bonds of association as race, religion, language, and ethnicity.

The history of the modern world might legitimately be written in terms of the master-theme of states making nations and nations striving to become states. In western Europe there have been two contrasting strands of development. In England and France, it is the story of the nation being forged over centuries through the activities of the state. Germany and Italy, on the other hand, emerged as states only after cultural and linguistic nationhood had been established. And in the western Europe of today we have both the strengthening of supranationalism *and* the assertion of cultural, linguistic, and other sub-national particularisms.[4] With it all, the demands of national self-determination remain in Europe and throughout the world the most persistent challenges to political stability, as Walker Connor points out:

> Ever since the abstract philosophical notion that the right to rule was vested in *the people* was first linked in popular fancy to a particular ethnically defined people—a development which first occurred at the time of the French Revolution—the conviction that one's own people should *not*, by the very nature of things, be ruled by those deemed aliens has proved to be a potent challenger to the legitimacy of multinational structures. As a consequence of this wedding of popular sovereignty to ethnicity…the political legitimacy of any state falling short of actual nation-statehood would become suspect to a segment or segments of its population.[5]

The demand for national self-determination has been accompanied by the distinctly modern notion that individual identity can be adequately realized only through a primary identification with the nation. René Lévesque expressed it this way in 1963:

> Every more or less clear-headed and open-eyed person surely knows that the nation is almost as vital to his balance and growth as the family. Denationalized, he becomes disoriented, incomplete, a member of an impoverished nation; a fearful nation, uncertain of everything including itself; he is thus degraded. Within a dynamic nation, on the contrary, he feels magnified, prouder and stronger.[6]

Charles Taylor in a recent essay describes the preconditions of what he designates as 'emancipated humanism' in these terms. 'For each man to discover in himself what his humanity consists in, he needs a horizon of meaning, which can only be by some allegiance, group membership, cultural tradition. He needs in the broadest sense a language in which to ask and answer the question of ultimate significance.'[7] The late Rupert Emerson thus described the modern condition:

> The nation is today the largest community which, when the chips are down, effectively commands man's loyalty, overriding the chances both of the lower communities within it and those which cut across it or potentially enfold it within a still greater society, reaching ultimately to mankind as a whole. In this sense the nation can be called a 'terminal community' with the implication that it is for present purposes the effective end of the road for man as a social animal, the end point of working solidarity between men.[8]

The crucial point here is not the nation in the cultural/linguistic sense as 'terminal community' but rather the linkage of ethnicity to statehood, the linkage that asserts that culture and language are the appropriate determinants of political allegiance and political organization. Benjamin Akzin writes that an ethnic group becomes a nation when it 'exercises in fact or effectually strives to exercise major influence on the political structure of society.'[9] Within this definition, an ethnic group without becoming a nation may act like other interest groups in trying to win concessions for its members such as, for example, education in the national language or non-discrimination against nationals in political, social, and economic life. It becomes a nation when it asserts either the control over a limited range of governmental matters or the possession of the full panoply of powers of the sovereign state.

The marriage of ethnicity and political organization is ultimately related to the expansion of the sphere of the governmental to include virtually every aspect of human life. Prior to modern times, nations in the cultural/ethnic/linguistic sense persisted and even thrived within the framework of multinational dynasties and empires. This is less possible with the existing scope of governmental activity. In contemporary debate about the growth of government we have been preoccupied with the economic to the neglect of what one might loosely designate as the social. Yet it is perhaps this latter that is more crucial to the stability of states comprehending more than one cultural/linguistic nation-state: activities related to family life, the mass media, cultural development, leisure, health, and so on. With the extension of the governmental come other organizations operating within political boundaries—Canadians are associated together not only for governmental purposes but as Presbyterians, trade unionists, mathematicians, fly fishermen, and so on. Under these conditions cultural nations, or those who claim to speak for them, can assert plausibly if not conclusively that national integrity and survival require a very wide range of state powers under the nation's control if not sovereignty in its most complete sense. Further, because the rewards inherent in the possession of state power are higher than in the past, national élites have more incentives than before to politicize ethnicity.

A recent impetus to national self-determination has been given by the fact that nations that are very small in population have now attained sovereignty. Connor has written that in the propaganda of Welsh nationalism it is frequently pointed out that an independent Wales would have more people than some thirty-nine independent states including Iceland, Luxembourg, and New Zealand.[10] A.H. Birch argues that 'since the Second World War, the balance of advantage between the sizeable multipurpose state and the small community has changed to the disadvantage of the sizeable state.'[11] The major factors in this changing balance are that 'the size of a country's population has ceased to bear a close relation to its military security' and that the development of supranational organizations has conferred on citizens of small states economic advantages previously available only to those of larger ones. Birch goes on to suggest that in today's world the way in which the boundaries of sovereign states are drawn is less consequential than before, and suggests that the levels of interdependence and integration now prevailing between the United Kingdom and Eire have been little affected by the latter's becoming a sovereign state in 1922. In general, then, the size barrier to national self-determination has gone.

What is the relation between the principle of national self-determination and the cultural/linguistic minorities comprehended within the boundaries of national states? In his essay 'Representative Government' John Stuart Mill asserted the democratic credentials of the principle thus: 'Where the sentiment of nationality exists in any force, there is a *prima facie* case for uniting all the members of the nationality under the same government, and a government to themselves apart. This is merely saying that the question of government ought to be decided by the governed.' Mill, like his friend and colleague Lord Durham, did not believe that what Mill elsewhere in the essay called the 'fellow-feeling' and 'unified public opinion' necessary to free government were possible when more than one group existed within the same state; when two or more groups were constrained to do so the solution was assimilationist. But apart from assimilation, the national state must inevitably assign minorities a subordinate role. In his lengthy study on the legal aspects of Quebec's accession to sovereignty Jacques Brossard attempts, unsuccessfully I think, to reconcile national self-determination with liberal principles.[12] Brossard argues that the right of a 'people' to self-determination as embodied in international law and convention is restricted to a group defined in cultural/linguistic terms. In the Quebec context this principle will appropriately be asserted by way of a popular referendum or plebiscite. But those citizens of Quebec who are not francophones have no right to participate in this decision, as francophones outside Quebec have not the right to participate in the parallel decision of the Canadian nation. It might, however, be prudent to allow the non-francophones of Quebec to cast votes in the plebiscite so that their sentiments about the matter were ascertained, although these ballots would be counted separately from those of Québécois. In the plebiscite each citizen would have the right to define himself as a francophone or non-francophone as he chose. This would appear from Brossard's argument to be an irrevocable choice which would subsequently determine his treatment—most crucially in respect to linguistic matters—as a member of the Quebec majority or minority. But the prior right of national self-determination can be demanded only by members of the majority as defined by culture and language.

The broad question then is whether the stable and desirable political community must be based on what has been called 'non-political similarity or similarities between men'.[13] Is the stable multinational state possible in a world in which, according to Connor's estimate, fewer than ten per cent of all states contain only one ethnic group? Let us look at this broader question in Canadian terms.

Unlike the founders of the American republic, the politicians of
Canada have never had the alternative of fashioning a political
community from the human materials of a people united by religion, common ancestry, language, manners, and morals. In the
Province of Canada during the period before Confederation, the
impulse to assimilate the French which was the underpinning of
both the Durham Report and the Act of Union was soon put in
abeyance—it is unlikely that the English-Canadian politicians
ever had much faith in either the workability or the desirability of
such assimilation. During the two decades after 1840 practices
developed very much along the lines of what contemporary students of politics call consociationalism.[14] These included some
recognition of the double-majority principle by which a measure
impinging on one of the two sections would come into effect only
after a majority from that section assented to it; political-party
groupings confined to one section; ministries headed by one leader
from Canada West and one from Canada East; the bifurcation of
several of the executive departments; the perambulation of the
capital before 1857 between Upper and Lower Canadian cities.
However, these devices did not on balance contribute to English-
French accommodation. J.M.S. Careless wrote of the United Province in the mid-1850s: 'Yet for all the quasi-federal structures in
Canada, there was no effective separation of sectional from common concerns within the single legislature. The cumbersome
expedient had frequently confused the two, and so made for angry
friction. Certainly Upper or Lower Canadians tended to adopt the
view that the province was one, or two, just as the occasion suited
them. . . . If quasi-federalism was a response to duality, it aggra-
vated rather than resolved inherent Canadian differences.'[15] As
time went on, the increasing insistence of Upper Canadians on
'rep. by pop.' brought deadlock to the province and a direct challenge to the régime of emergent consociationalism.

The Confederation settlement of 1864-7 hammered out between
the British North American politicians and embodied in its main
features in the British North America Act of 1867 attempted to
effect a very new solution in the relationship between cultural
nationhood and political organization. The Fathers of Confederation explicitly put aside both the assimilationist premises of the
Act of Union and the consociational devices which had developed

as a response to the persistence of English-French duality. More specifically, the Confederation settlement included four sets of provisions bearing directly on culture, language, and religion. First, and perhaps most crucially, legislative jurisdiction in respect to matters where English and French differed most profoundly was conferred on the provinces—most importantly of course on French-dominated Quebec. Provincial jurisdiction thus included education, property and civil rights, the solemnization of marriage, control over what we would now designate as health and welfare, and municipal institutions.

Second, the French Canadians were given certain protections in the operation of the institutions of the Dominion. Section 133 provided for the use of both languages in the Parliament of Canada and in courts established by Parliament. Perhaps more importantly, it was decided in 1866 that the Dominion cabinet be constituted with regard for representation from Quebec and the other provinces; although such representation was not embodied explicitly in law, it became from the first and remained a convention of the Canadian constitution.

Third, the English-speaking minority of Quebec was granted several explicit protections. Section 133 provided for the two languages in the legislature of Quebec and in Quebec courts and for representation of this minority in the Senate of Canada and the Quebec legislative assembly. Fourth, Section 93 gave protection to the educational rights of Protestant and Roman Catholic minorities in the provinces against provincial majorities. If these rights were encroached upon, the Dominion cabinet was given the authority to intervene to safeguard them and, as a last resort, Parliament might enact remedial legislation.

Insofar as the cultural element of the Confederation settlement was given an explicit defence, this was made by George-Étienne Cartier in the Confederation Debates of 7 February 1865. He said:

In ancient times, the manner in which a nation grew up was very different from that of the present day. Then the first weak settlement increased into a village, which, by turns, became a town and a city, and the nucleus of a nation. It was not so in modern times. Nations were now formed by the agglomeration of communities having kindred interests any sympathies. Such was our case at the present moment. Objection had been taken to the scheme now under consideration, because of the words 'new nationality'. Now when we were united together, if union were attained, we would form a political nationality with which neither the national origin, nor the religion of any individual would interfere. It was lamented by some that we had this, and hopes were expressed that this distinctive feature would cease. The idea of unity of races was utopian—it was impossible. Distinctions of this kind would always exist. Dissimilarity, in fact, appeared to be the order of the physical world and of the moral world, as well as in the political world.[16]

So far as the two major communities were concerned Cartier said, 'Under the Federation scheme, granting those large questions of general interest in which the differences of race or religion had no place, it could not be pretended that the rights of either race or religion could be invaded at all.'[17] He was also sanguine that there would be no encroachment on the rights of Protestant and Roman Catholic minorities in the provinces because this 'would be censured everywhere'.

Not even the most fervent admirer of Cartier would assert that he was a profound political thinker, and it is thus imprudent to read too much coherence into his view of political nationality. But perhaps he was saying something like this. Being a Canadian is exclusively a political matter and neither a person's political rights nor his political obligations should be influenced by his cultural/religious/linguistic affiliations or allegiances. In institutional terms, matters of direct cultural incidence are under provincial jurisdiction while those general matters of no such incidence are conferred on the Dominion. Whatever cleavages develop in respect to these latter will not divide Canadians on cultural/linguistic/religious axes.

Cartier's version of a Canadian political nationality was *not* realized in the subsequent history of the Dominion.

First, Canadians of British antecedents denied people of other extractions an equal role in Canadian affairs. The relatively relaxed 'Little Englandism' which had prevailed in both British North America and the United Kingdom itself at the time of Confederation gave way in the next quarter-century to a master-race imperialism which reached its zenith perhaps at the time of the First World War. As Carl Berger has so well demonstrated, an important, if not the dominant, variant of Canadian nationalism was imperialist.[18] At least until the end of the Second World War those of the dominant charter-group associated Britishness and Protestantism with being Canadian in the fullest sense of the word, and in a host of ways people of French and other national origins were relegated to a subordinate place in Canadian affairs.

Second, the Dominion authorities failed to secure religious and linguistic duality against provincial majorities. The English-speaking minority in Quebec had ample economic power to safeguard its own interests. It was a different matter with the French and Catholic minorities of the other provinces. From the refusal of the Dominion cabinet to disallow New Brunswick legislation of the early 1870s challenging the privileges of Catholic and French-language schools, Ottawa was never willing to take effective action to safeguard cultural/linguistic/religious duality against English-speaking and Protestant provincial majorities. W. L. Morton has made a persuasive argument that this failure contributed to French Canadians' being thrown back on the Quebec state alone as the exclusive bulwark of their national rights, and that it is at the root of the most critical strains in Confederation today.[19]

Third, the federal government extended its powers to include matters of a direct cultural incidence. This general development took place most dramatically in the quarter-century after the Second World War with Ottawa's involvement, mainly through the exercise of the federal spending power, in a host of matters which were in a general sense within provincial legislative jurisdiction: health, social assistance, housing, post-secondary education, cultural development, broadcasting, athletics, and so on.

The most critical challenge to Confederation in the past two decades has come from a modern and modernizing Quebec in which a new francophone élite has turned to the Quebec state as the protector of national rights and interests. Hubert Guindon has made a powerful argument that the basic social compact of Confederation was a 'tacit agreement' between 'the English merchant class of Montreal and the Catholic clergy in Quebec'.[20] According to this agreement, the Church's legitimacy would no longer be challenged by the Crown and further attempts to assimilate French Canadians would cease. Also, 'The trade-off for the preservation of language and religion was the complete institutional and educational autonomy of the English, and exclusion from partnership in the industrial capitalist enterprise. Put more bluntly, the trade-off was between religion and language and economic subordination or underdevelopment.[21] This compact broke down with the post-1960 modernization of Quebec and the consequent destruction of the power of one of the parties to it, the Catholic hierarchy of Quebec.

Let us now turn our attention to the response of other Canadians to the new Quebec. I am not here primarily concerned with either popular attitudes or such changes in public policy as the Official Languages Act and the accommodations to Quebec effected through federal-provincial negotiation. Rather, I shall focus in the rest of this paper on a broad and amorphous ideological reformulation of Canada and the Canadian experience made by English-speaking intellectuals in the past two decades. I shall designate this broad current of opinion as 'dualist revisionism'. In my view, the most distinguished expressions of dualist revisionism are in the writings of Gad Horowitz and Abraham Rotstein, and I rely heavily on these writings in what I have to say.

From the early 1960s onward there has been an enhanced disposition among the intellectual élites of English-speaking Canada to emphasize cultural duality in the Canadian experience. David R. Cameron has succinctly described this perspective: 'Dualism in Canada may generally be described as the view which holds that the most significant cleavage in Canadian society is the line dividing English from French, and which identifies as the major challenge to domestic statecraft the establishment of harmonious and just relations between the English-speaking and French-speaking communities of Canada.'[22] Ramsay Cook summed it up even more pithily in the introduction to his book *Canada and the French-Canadian Question*: 'Canada and the French-Canadian question is really the Canadian question.'[23] The impetus to look at Canada in this way was derived in part from the activities of the Royal Commission on Bilingualism and Biculturalism which provided scholars with research funds at unprecedented levels, and from the coming to power in 1968 of a prime minister whose abiding preoccupation was French-English relations. In the light of the new perspectives, which almost all of us to a degree share, it seems remarkable how insensitive was the previous generation of English-Canadian scholars (most notably, perhaps, Angus, Brady, Creighton, Corry, Dawson, Innis, and Underhill) to the dualistic dimension of the Canadian experience—Arthur Lower and Frank Scott were exceptions.

Beyond the general disposition to emphasize the French-English dimension of the Canadian experience, dualist revisionism has been characterized by four interrelated elements which are more specific.

First, there is a benevolent view of the new Quebec and a readiness to accept the claims of Quebec nationalists on other Canadians. In an article published in 1971, Rotstein asserted his support for a new political formula based on the proposition that 'Quebec has the absolute right to self-determination up to and including independence.'[24] The general disposition of revisionists is to regard the nationalists of Quebec as the authentic spokesmen of that community and either to challenge or to ignore contrary currents of Quebec opinion, specifically those of Pierre Elliott Trudeau and such federalist scholars as Roger Dehem, Gilles Lalande, and Maurice Pinard.

Secondly, there is an obsession with American power and an urgency that English Canadians constitute themselves as a nation to resist that power in its cultural, economic, military, and other dimensions. There is a pervasive influence of the writings of Louis Hartz on this revisionist current, with his portrayal of the United States as a nation irrevocably based on a homogeneous set of liberal values. The differentiation between Canada and the United States and the credentials of Canadian and/or English-Canadian nationhood are founded on the persistence in Canada of non-liberal values, and the ideological imperative is to emphasize these values. This thrust has several variants. Herschel Hardin has made an ingenious attempt to locate Canadian-American differentiation in the 'Canadian public enterprise culture'.[25] Proceeding from the analysis of the late Karl Polanyi, Rotstein sees nationalism and the nation-state as defensive instruments against the community-destroying processes of modernization.[26] Horowitz follows the Hartzian framework more explicitly in emphasizing the persistence of Tory and socialist fragments in Canada. The anti-liberal ideological community in Canada is indeed an inclusive one. The complimentary Foreword to the 1977 book *The Liberal Idea of Canada*[27] by James Laxer and Robert Laxer, two writers in the Marxist tradition, was written by the conservative

Christian scholar George Grant. The accompanying publisher's blurb contains testimonies to the excellence of the Laxers' analysis by Rotstein, Dalton Camp, and the late Donald Creighton.

Thirdly, English Canada is at least potentially a nation and it is imperative that it should constitute itself as such. Only by doing so can English Canada establish a constructive and harmonious relationship with Quebec and act effectively to resist American power. Rotstein so wrote in a 1978 article: 'if a vigorous nationalism in Quebec is actually now the chief political force in the province ... it follows we must have in Canada two nationalisms rather than one. Quebec nationalism in my view must have its broad counterpart in English-speaking Canada with whom it can communicate in a common "language", a partner that could understand and articulate the same goals of cultural, political and economic self-determination.'[28] Horowitz has been more explicit than other revisionists in his prescriptions for the organizational forms that the two nations should take: 'We must have the courage to combine *accommodation* of the French particularism with *resistance* to intra-English particularisms.'[29]

These, then, are the broad elements of dualist revisionism. To varying degrees intellectuals in this broad current of opinion are self-consciously attempting an ideological reformulation of Canadian experience and Canadian possibilities to convince the rest of us to think and act in ways different from hitherto. An ideology is an admixture of an explanation of some existing state of social, political, and economic circumstances, a strategy for either changing or preserving that state of affairs, and a call to action to undertake the recommended strategy. Thus a particular ideology may appropriately be evaluated in terms of the adequacy of its explanation, the feasibility of its strategy, and its capacity to inspire action.

Dualist revisionism has on the whole failed to change the ways that most Canadians think and act in relation to the political community. The most dramatic demonstration of this failure has been the adverse public reaction among English-speaking Canadians to the two-nations view of Canada with which both the Progressive Conservatives and the New Democrats flirted a decade ago. In part, perhaps, this rejection of the two-nations doctrine can be explained in terms of sheer anti-French bigotry. In part, too, there was the understandable apprehension of people whose ethnic origins were neither English nor French to a 'two founding races' view, which made their credentials as Canadians ambiguous at best. Yet perhaps other explanations can be given.

First, the ongoing territorial separation of English-speaking and French-speaking Canadians means that a decreasing proportion of Canadians experience duality as an important circumstance of daily life.[30] The human implications of these demographic trends have been much neglected—on a day-to-day and a week-to-week basis most citizens have little direct contact with members of the other linguistic community. Because of this, the resistance of most non-francophones to a view that the essential nature of their country is dualistic is understandable, even when this resistance is expressed in such ungenerous sentiments as those of people not wanting French to be forced down their throats when demonstrably no one is trying to do any such thing.

Second, and this point is closely related to the first, the balance of population and power is shifting towards a region in which dualism has few roots. This westward shift is more than economic and political and is resulting, and will increasingly result, in reformulations of Canada and the Canadian experience compatible with Western interests and attitudes.[31] It is trite to say that dualism has not been an essential element of the Western experience.

Third, even if English Canada is indeed a nation it has no political instruments for the expression of its collective will. The federal government cannot be such an instrument because it is shared with Québécois, and the governments of the provinces with English-speaking majorities have little disposition to act in concert. To recommend, as does Horowitz, that English Canada be constituted on quasi-unitary lines defies both past experience and current realities. Further, the circumstance that neither the Progressive Conservatives nor the New Democrats receive effective electoral support from Quebec has not led these parties to define themselves as manifestations of English Canada alone.

In terms of analysis and explanation, dualist revisionism proceeds from gross distortions of the three entities with which it concerns itself: Quebec, the United States, and English-speaking Canada.

As we have seen, revisionism has a pervasive disposition to regard Quebec nationalism as the only legitimate and authentic expression of the views and interests of that community. Yet Quebec remains ideologically divided in its responses to the national question and to its relations with the wider Canadian community. It does on the whole seem illogical for non-Quebeckers to assert the right of Quebec to national self-determination and then to deny the authenticity of the views of federalist Quebeckers as a legitimate expression of the will and interests of Quebec.

The revisionist view of the United States is also questionable. S. F. Wise has written about Canadian opinions of the United States between 1837 and 1867: 'the Canadian picture of American institutions had little to do with objective reality.... On the whole, the judgments of Canadians upon American political phenomena were not judgments at all in any rational sense, but rather were ritualistic expressions of deeply held assumptions, responses triggered by danger signals from the south that their political culture had conditioned them to recognize.'[32] Significantly, Canadian revisionists almost never refer to what sophisticated contemporary Americanists, apart from Louis Hartz, have written about the United States. It appears to me that there is a perspective on liberalism here that is both superficial and malevolent and that vastly exaggerates the extent to which liberalism has overcome the communitarian and conservative elements of American life—for example, the strong tradition of private philanthropy, the continuing strength and vitality of the complex of private colleges and universities, the pervasive localism of much of political and social life, and the persistence of ethnicity, which increasingly engages the attention of serious students of American society. It is, on the whole, peculiar to have a nation depicted as irretrievably liberal when the most decisive of its experiences was the defeat of one of its regions in its aspirations for self-determination and the subsequent re-establishment of the national community on the profoundly organic principle of 'an indestructible union, composed of indestructible states'.[33] And it is doubly strange when those who see the United States as homogeneously liberal go on both to hymn the praises of the alleged organic-Tory foundations of Canadian life and *then* to assert the voluntarist, un-Tory, unorganic principle of Quebec's right to self-determination.

But dualist revisionism is a call to action directed towards English-speaking Canadians. What then is the bond of English-Canadian nationhood? It obviously cannot be language alone because this is shared with Americans and other peoples. In some of the revisionist writings it appears that the major impulse to English-Canadian nationhood should be to interact more constructively with Quebec. Yet it seems to me patently unrealistic to expect the larger of the two communities to change its organization and ideology for the sole reason that this will bring about better relations with the smaller. To use an analogy which is not totally misleading, the cause of Christian ecumenicism might well be furthered if the denominations of the World Council of Churches united themselves under a common hierarchy which would associate with the Vatican. Yet if Baptists or Presbyterians consented to this they would cease in any definable way to be Baptists or Presbyterians because these traditions are in large part centred on ecclesiastical organization. So it is with English- and French-speaking Canada. But in most of the revisionists' handiwork the chief bond of English-Canadian nationhood appears to be ideology. Within the Hartzian framework there is an emphasis on the Tory and socialist fragments and the differentiation from American liberalism. Gad Horowitz put it this way: 'English Canada is not worth preserving unless it can be different from the United States. Our British past provides the foundation for building on the northern half of the continent a social democratic order (let Grant call it conservative if he wishes) *better* than the liberal society of the United States.'[34] Notice here the equation of social democracy with conservatism. As is well known, Horowitz has conjured up almost single-handedly the position of 'red Toryism' which permits such a powerful thinker as George Grant to avoid coming to terms with the conflicting views of socialism and conservatism about equality, and permits Dalton Camp to state that he wishes he himself had written the neo-Marxist analysis of Canada by the Laxers.[35]

There are other defects in the revisionists' view:

First, they minimize the continuing liberalization of Canadian life, particularly in the period since the Second World War. S. D. Clark has more convincingly than anyone else analysed the anti-liberal elements in Canadian development[36] and has attributed these, accurately I believe, to the nature of the Canadian frontier. Thus,

It was upon a very narrow economic base that the Canadian community was built. Canada has been what the late H. A. Innis called a 'hard frontier'. The exploitation of her resources has required large accumulations of capital, corporate forms of business enterprise, and state support. In the structure of its economic life, the country as a whole has had much of the character of a single enterprise community.[36]

Also, 'before the Second World War, the Canadian society had very much the character of a social mosaic. The assimilative forces of the urban middle class structure extended only a very little beyond the bounds of the tight little urban complexes that housed the middle class society.'[37] But, according to Clark's analysis, many of these boundaries to mobility have recently crumbled or are in process of doing so.[38] Wallace Clement's recent findings about the persistence of ascriptive criteria in the recruitment and advancement of members of the Canadian economic élite is a necessary corrective to any analysis suggesting that liberalization has triumphed.[39] However, in the complex of federal and provincial human-rights legislation, and in federal provisions eschewing racial or ethnic criteria in the selection of immigrants to Canada, there is at least a symbolic commitment to liberalism and to universalistic standards. I believe the effects are more than symbolic. And old-stock Canadians, particularly those of British origin, increasingly accept the attainment by individuals from other backgrounds of positions of status and power in various aspects of Canadian life. Second, revisionists tend to sentimentalize the actual and possible role of public action. The role of the state in Canadian economic development is a hugely complex matter. It is inappropriate to follow a crude Marxism in perceiving all actions of the state as manifestations of the power of the bourgeoisie exercised in a direct and straightforward way. Yet we should not be sentimental. Hardin's elaboration and defence of the Canadian 'public enterprise culture' passes over the ambiguities of public enterprise in Canada, particularly the extent to which such activities have been guided by market rather than public-interest standards. Rotstein is notably imprecise in elaborating the capacity of the authorities of the nation-state to forestall the community-destroying effects of multinational corporations. Those on the moderate left of the Canadian political spectrum are just now beginning to realize that the extension of the public sector has no inevitable disposition to further communitarian and egalitarian values. In their book *Political Parties in Canada*, Conrad Winn and John McMenemey supply the necessary corrective:

> The philosophical cornerstones of the Canadian left are social equality and governmental intervention. The philosophical cornerstones of the Canadian right are autonomy from government and the rewarding of private effort. From intellectual weakness and sometimes from electoral self-interest as well, both the left and the right have failed to set the parameters or criteria by which the growth of the public sector is to be assessed. Thus the civil service has been free to satisfy the sometimes indiscriminate public demand for government services and bureaucratic desires for empire-building. The left has been content to accept government intervention on the assumption that government intervention somehow assures social equality. The right has been prepared to set aside its predilections against government activity on the knowledge that its natural constituency, the middle and upper strata, is confident that it can receive a sizeable share of government beneficence.[40]

This summary account is, I believe, more accurate than those analyses which are disposed to emphasize almost exclusively the communitarian and egalitarian impact of state activity.

Let us return to the major focus of this essay which is the relation between culture and political organization. English-speaking Canadians have in recent years been unwilling to accept the revisionist formula that political community should be established on the basis of culture/language/ethnicity. On the whole I regard this rejection as fortunate. But is there an alternative formula more compatible with our historical experiences and present circumstances? I would suggest in a somewhat tentative fashion that there has been a recrudescence of Cartier's vision of a Canadian political nationality. This is the argument of a much neglected essay of Kenneth McNaught, published in 1966, in which he asserts that 'English-speaking Canadians take a non-racial view of nationality.'[41] With the decline of British imperial power and the decreasing proportion of Canadians with familial and other direct links to the United Kingdom there is a weakening of the disposition to associate national origins with the political and other dimensions of full membership in the Canadian community; there was a surprising lack of resistance, even from those most directly affected, to legislative measures of a decade ago which abolished political privileges of British citizens not possessed by other aliens. As we have seen, legislation prohibits ethnic, racial, and other ascriptive criteria in various aspects of Canadian life; significantly, minority groups in Canada have been less disposed to press for affirmative action than have their American counterparts. John Diefenbaker's allegiance to the notion of 'unhyphenated Canadianism' has had a good deal of support. And it is not without significance that Canada's largest city, which was formerly the bastion of Anglo-Saxon and Tory values, has become almost inordinately proud of its cosmopolitan and multicultural nature.[42]

Political nationality is thus a matter of 'limited identity', to use J.M.S. Careless's term.[43] Each individual is enmeshed in a matrix of associations, each performing specific and limited functions. Under the best of all circumstances the person's institutional allegiances are complementary rather than competitive, and this condition can be met only when such institutions confine their demands by voluntary self-restraint and/or are confined by various kinds of checks and balances. Some commitment to the political order is of course required to legitimate the demands that this order makes on citizens. Yet political nationality as I understand it explicitly rejects the notions that in any a priori sense political allegiance overrides all other affiliations and that the fulfilled and emancipated person must regard the national polity as the 'terminal community'.

But if English-speaking Canadians have come to emphasize the non-cultural view of nationality more than in the past, will this not inevitably mean a stand-off with Québécois who assert the primacy of culture and language in political organization and allegiance? Perhaps. William Kilbourn wrote in 1967 that 'the old unhyphenated Canadianism ... is simply a continuation in milder form of English-Canadian imperialism',[44] and will inevitably be regarded by French Canadians as such. Charles Taylor has made a sophisticated argument that under conditions of 'emancipated humanism' persons will be disposed to identify only with political communities founded on a common language.[45]

One might, however, posit circumstances under which Québécois would be disposed to accept a view of political nationality divorced from language/culture/ethnicity. I make no firm judgement about how likely this is to occur. One of the crucial elements here is the creation of political nationality within Quebec itself. Perhaps as Québécois become increasingly relaxed and confident about their own society and as non-francophone Québécois come to terms with their new circumstances, Quebec society and politics will come decreasingly to revolve around cleavages of culture and language. And political nationality in the wider Canadian sense might come through successful and continuing efforts to strengthen the participation of Québécois in various aspects of Canadian life, most crucially of course in the operations of the federal government.

My tempered optimism that some considerable commitment among Québécois to political nationality is possible has been strengthened by a reading of the document *A New Canadian Federation* issued by Claude Ryan and his colleagues in January 1980.[46] I refer here mainly to the ideological formulations of the first and last chapters of this document rather than to its specific recommendations for institutional reform. Interestingly and significantly, the NCF paper in its opening paragraphs links its viewpoint explicitly with a tradition of Canadian federalism derived from the Quebec Fathers of Confederation. The report eschews such terminology as that of 'two nations' or 'special status' which connote that French-English duality is *the* central reality of the Canadian experience to which all other considerations must give way. The NCF document *does* provide for duality but, like the Confederation settlement, specifies the requirements of duality in very specific terms: the constitutional entrenchment of linguistic rights, the provision for a 'dualist committee' of the Federal Council with responsibilities related to cultural and linguistic measures, the recommendation providing for a 'dualist constitutional bench' in certain constitutional disputes. Near the end of the paper it is asserted that allegiances to Quebec and Canada are fully compatible.

We refuse to choose between Quebec and Canada. On the contrary, we choose Quebec AND Canada because each one needs the other to fulfill itself. We are convinced that one can, at the same time, be an authentic Quebecer and an authentic Canadian.[47]

But in my view the recrudescence of Canadian political nationality is a necessary but not a sufficient condition of the re-establishment of the Canadian Confederation. The other precondition is in the form of limitations on the powers of the federal and provincial governments, particularly as these powers impinge directly on language and culture. With the present scope of the public sector, it is inevitable that ethnicity will be politicized and that jurisdictions will extend the rights of first-class citizenship either to one culture alone or to the cultures that receive official recognition. I realize that this general prescription is contrary to prevailing currents of thought and policies on both the Canadian communities which define culture broadly and assert a pervasive role for the public authorities in its defence. For example, the Quebec White Paper on cultural development published in 1978 defines culture to include, among other things, scientific research, leisure, the mass media, arts and letters, housing, health, and architecture as well as public education as more narrowly designated, and proposes an interventionist policy by the Quebec government in respect to all these fields of human activity.[48] Bill 101 regulates the use of language in Quebec in a more comprehensive and detailed way than does any other jurisdiction in the Western world. There are parallel dispositions in English-speaking Canada, justified for the most part on the basis of a resistance to American influence and values. Rotstein has written, 'America is total environment, it envelops us as a mist, penetrating every sphere of our cultural, political, economic, and social environment.'[49] And to resist this total environment it is of course judged necessary to erect a total and inevitably statist response.

I confess not to have examined in any detailed way the implications of my general prescription. Its general thrust is somehow to restore the influence of voluntary associations and to remove them from government patronage and influence. Members of the artistic, scholarly, and scientific communities in Canada are only now awakening, and very belatedly, to the fact that state support of their activities inevitably compromises freedom of expression. A few of us are increasingly concerned with state control of leisure time and recreation. Apart from individual entrepreneurs in a few such sports as golf and tennis, serious athletic competition is more and more between the hired guns of either big business or national governments. Such examples might be multiplied, but the general argument still stands that the stability and legitimacy of a multi-cultural society is challenged by a range of state activity in which ethnicity is increasingly politicized.

My general commitments are thus liberal. Liberalism receives a bad press in Canada and I find that among even the most thought-ful of our graduate students this ideology is known almost entirely through the writings of such hostile critics as Macpherson and Grant, which is akin to studying the Indians with exclusive reliance on the diaries of Daniel Boone or Catholic theology with-out proceeding beyond the writings of Voltaire. I have less regard for the Tory elements of the Canadian past than do some of my colleagues, I see few inherent possibilities in them for bringing about a socialist future, and I have little enthusiasm for restoring titles in Canada or strengthening such ailing organizations as the Monarchist League, the Loyal Orange Order, and the United Empire Loyalist Association. I suspect that there is a more com-plex relation between liberalism and nationalism than the English-Canadian revisionists suppose, but in any direct clash between the two sets of values I shall unhesitatingly choose liberal-ism. The long-run danger to Canadian nationhood as I see it lies not in our corruption by American liberal values but in the weak-ening of the tradition of liberalism within the United States itself.

NOTES

1. For a collection of papers whose major focus is on the relation between modern-ization and ethnicity see Milton J. Esman, ed., *Ethnic Conflict in the Western World* (Ithaca, 1977). See particularly Esman's concluding essay, 'Perspectives in Ethnic Conflict in Industrialized Societies', pp. 371-80.

2. See Dale Posgate and Kenneth McRoberts, *Quebec: Social Change in Political Crisis* (Toronto, 1976) for an analysis centred on the concept of modernization. A second edition of this book by McRoberts alone is to be published in 1980.

3. The best general analysis of national self-determination I know is Alfred Cob-ban, *The Nation State and National Self-Determination*, ed. by Muriel Cobban (rev.

ed.; London and Glasgow, 1969). The writings of Walker Connor on ethnonationalism emphasize the origins in the French Revolution.

4. Lawrence Scheinemann, 'The Interface of Regionalism in Western Europe:
Brussels and the Perephines', in Esman, *Ethnic Conflict*, pp. 65-80.

5. 'Ethnonationalism in the First World: The Present in Historical Perspective',
in Esman, *Ethnic Conflict*, p. 25.

6. Translated from *Le Devoir* interview of 5 July 1963 in Frank Scott and Michael
Oliver, eds, *Quebec States Her Case* (Toronto, 1964), p. 134.

7. Charles Taylor, 'Why Do Nations Have to Become States?', in *Confederation:
Philosophers Look at Canadian Confederation* (Montreal, 1979), p. 24.

8. *From Empire to Nation: The Rise to Self-Assertion of Asian and African Peoples*
(Boston, 1966), pp. 95-6.

9. *States and Nations* (New York, 1966), p. 39.

10. 'Ethnonationalism', p. 31n.

11. 'Minority Nationalist Movements and Theories of Political Integration', *World
Politics*, XXX. April 1978, p. 335.

12. *L'Accession à la souveraineté et le cas du Québec* (Montreal, 1976), particularly pp.
356-65.

13. The phrase is from Anne Cohler, *Rousseau and Nationalism* (New York, 1970),
p. 4, as quoted in William Mathie, 'Political Community and the Canadian
Experience: Reflections in Nationalism, Federalism and Unity', *Canadian
Journal of Political Science*, XII. March 1979, p. 14.

14. Donald V. Smiley, *Canada in Question: Federalism in the Seventies*, 2nd ed.
(Toronto, 1976), pp. 138-40.

15. *The Union of the Canadas: The Growth of Canadian Institutions, 1841-1857*
(Toronto, 1967), p. 210.

16. *Parliamentary Debates on the Confederation of British North American Provinces*
(Ottawa, 1951), p. 60.

17. *Ibid.*

18. *The Sense of Power: Studies in the Ideas of Canadian Imperialism, 1867-1914*
(Toronto, 1970).

19. 'Confederation, 1870-1896: The End of the Macdonaldian Constitution and the
Return to Duality', in Bruce Hodgins and Robert Page, eds, *Canadian History
since 1867: Essays and Interpretations* (Georgetown, Ont., 1972), particularly pp.
195-200 and p. 208.

20. 'The Modernization of Quebec and the Legitimacy of the Canadian State' in
Daniel Glenday, Hubert Guindon, and Allan Turowetz, eds, *Modernization and
the Canadian State* (Toronto, 1978), p. 235.

21. *Ibid.*, p. 236.

22. 'Dualism and the Concept of National Unity' in John H. Redekop, ed.,
Approaches to Canadian Politics (Scarborough, 1978), p. 237.

23. *Canada and the French-Canadian Question* (Toronto, 1966), p. 2.

24. Abraham Rotstein, ed., *Power Corrupted: The October Crisis and the Repression of
Quebec* (Toronto, 1971), no pagination.

25. *A Nation Unaware: The Canadian Economic Culture* (North Vancouver, 1974),
particularly Part II. 'The Canadian Public Enterprise Culture'.

26. See generally *The Precarious Homestead* (Toronto, 1973).

27. *The Liberal Idea of Canada* (Toronto, 1977).
28. 'Is There an English-Canadian Nationalism?', *Journal of Canadian Studies* 13, Summer 1978, p. 115.
29. 'Mosaics and Identity', *Canadian Dimension* (reprint, n.d. [1966?]), p. 8.
30. For example, according to the 1971 census there were fifty-two urban municipalities in Canada with more than fifty thousand people and of these only eight had official-language minorities of more than ten per cent. Five of these were in the Montreal metropolitan area and the others were Sherbrooke, Sudbury, and Ottawa. On the demographic aspects of English and French in Canada, see Richard J. Jay, *Languages in Conflict* (Toronto, 1972) and Richard Arès, s. J., *Les Positions-ethniques, linguistiques et religieuses—des canadiens français à la suite du recensement de 1971* (Montreal, 1975).
31. For a lucid view of western attitudes, including those towards duality, see John Archer, 'The Prairie Perspective in 1977', in Richard Simeon, ed., *Must Canada Fail?* (Montreal, 1977), pp. 73-84.
32. 'The Annexation Movement and Its Effect on Canadian Public Opinion, 1837-1867', in S. F. Wise and Robert Craig Brown, eds, *Canada Views the United States: Nineteenth Century Political Attitudes* (Toronto, 1967), p. 95.
33. This often-quoted phrase was uttered by Chief Justice Salmon Chase in *Texas* v. *White*, decided by the Supreme Court of the United States in 1869.
34. 'Mosaics and Identity', p. 4, italics in text.
35. Publisher's advertisement for Laxer and Laxer, *The Liberal Idea of Canada*.
36. 'Capitalist Enterprise in Canadian Society', in S. D. Clark, *The Developing Canadian Community* (Toronto, 1962), p. 248.
37. 'Movements of Protest in Post-War Canadian Society', in S. D. Clark, *Canadian Society in Historical Perspective* (Toronto, 1976), p. 38.
38. *Ibid.*, pp. 38, 51.
39. *Continental Corporate Power: Economic Linkages between Canada and the United States* (Toronto, 1977), Chapter 7.
40. *Political Parties in Canada* (Toronto, 1976), p. 274.
41. 'The National Outlook of English-speaking Canadians', in Peter Russell, ed., *Nationalism in Canada*, (Toronto, 1966), pp. 61-71.
42. According to the 1971 census, 43.6 per cent of the residents of Toronto were born outside Canada, the largest proportion of foreign-born in Canada's twelve largest cities, and in marked contrast with 18.8 per cent in Montreal and 2.0 per cent in Quebec City.
43. 'Limited Identities in Canada', in *Canadian Historical Review*, March 1969, pp. 1-10.
44. Introduction to Paul G. Cornell, Jean Hamelin, Fernand Ouellet and Marcel Trudel, *Canada: Unity in Diversity* (Toronto, 1967), p. xi.
45. Taylor, 'Why do Nations Have to Become States'.
46. The Constitutional Committee of the Quebec Liberal Party, *A New Canadian Federation* (Montreal, 1980).
47. *Ibid.*, p. 140.
48. *La Politique québécoise du developpement culturel*, 2 vols (Quebec, 1978).
49. 'Bending Prometheus', in *The Precarious Homestead*, p. 183.

II
Canadiens and Canadians

Ramsay Cook

THE PARADOX OF QUEBEC

'What will finally become of French Canada? To tell the truth, no one really knows, especially not French Canadians, whose ambivalence on this topic is typical: they want simultaneously to give in to cultural fatigue and to overcome it, calling for renunciation and determination in the same breath.'
—HUBERT AQUIN, 'The Cultural Fatigue of French Canada' (1962)

I

'Canada is not a country,' the Quebec poet Jean-Guy Pilon wrote as he crossed the prairies heading for Vancouver in 1968, 'it's a continent washed by three oceans where twenty million people live, about one third of them French.... In these vast stretches of the Anglo-Saxon West I feel the difference inside me. I am definitely not at home and I realize how true it is to say that Quebec is an entity unto itself with its own culture, language, way of life.'[1] But having affirmed his distinctiveness Pilon went on to wonder if, and for how long, that difference could be preserved. 'What will become of it?' he queried, and suggested that the answer be postponed for another ten years.

It is that very ambiguity about the future that has long characterized Quebec and makes French Canadians a paradox for most of us. The same electorate that gave René Lévesque, an avowed *souverainiste*, provincial power on 15 November 1976 gave Pierre-Elliott Trudeau, an avowed federalist, even stronger support on 18 February 1980. One of Quebec's greatest artists, Paul-Émile Borduas, declared about twenty years ago, 'I hate all nationalisms.'[2] Today most Quebec artists and writers would probably insist that nationalism was what inspired their work. Yet even in a society where many of the leading intellectuals are proclaimed *indépendantistes*, two young philosophers recently published a book, *Le Territoire imaginaire de la culture*,³ rejecting the nationalist identification of state and nation on which the Lévesque government's policies rest. That the paradox, the ambiguity, is there is readily demonstrated. It is the most striking result of opinion surveys on the independence question and Parti Québécois support.⁴ One nationalist insists that 'we must resolve it now or resign ourselves to destruction.'⁵ Another, quite accurately seeing sovereignty-association as part of the ambiguity, wonders 'if the nationalist movement is not in an irretrievable process of dissolution'.⁶

In the face of this paradox, how can an English Canadian be expected to decipher the riddle of the face of the French-speaking sphinx? For nearly twenty-five years I have been trying, and I must confess that some of the message still eludes me. Recently several writers have tried to extract the secret by the use of codes supplied by Karl Marx, Albert Memmi, Jurgen Habermas, Nicos Pouzlantzas, Louis Althusser, among others.⁷ The results, to say the least, are confusing. Is the sphinx bourgeois or merely petit-bourgeois? Is the class struggle nationalist or anti-nationalist? These are intriguing questions, but until they are settled perhaps there is still some value in an approach that tries to understand what is on Quebeckers' minds by listening to what they have had to say over time. Let me begin at a period of severe crisis in French Canada's history.

II

Eighteen forty was a grim year for French Canadians. Papineau's abortive rebellion and its aftermath had left the *Canadiens* profoundly pessimistic. Durham's *Report*, recommending assimilation, had an air of finality about it. Union with Upper Canada, as the essential first step, was about to be forced on Lower Canada. So bleak was the future that Étienne Parent, the most brilliant political writer of his generation and editor of the nationalist *Le Canadien*, declared his acceptance of assimilation if that was the price necessary to gain responsible government.⁸

In that depressed atmosphere of 1840, two *Canadien* artists set down, one in poetry, the other in paint, their convictions and feelings about the future. In doing so they provided two enduring

clues to the well-springs of nationalism among French Canadians.
The poet was François-Xavier Garneau, later to become famous as
a historian. In 1840 he published 'The Last Huron', a poem about
a people who had been defeated, dispersed, and assimilated.

> Their names, their eyes, their festivals, their history
> Lie in the grave with them forever,
> And I alone remain to speak of them
> To the people of our day![9]

The Hurons, of course, stood as symbols for *Canadiens* who, Garneau feared, would share the fate of that once proud and powerful
Indian nation.

An Indian also served as a symbol of French Canada in Joseph
Légaré's 1840 painting entitled *Paysage au Monument à Wolfe*. Here
we see the Indian apparently offering to surrender his bow to the
statue of the conqueror, General James Wolfe. Yet nearby, hidden
behind a tree-trunk, is a canoe waiting to carry the Indian away to
his freedom. The critics seem agreed that the Indian (a Mercury
figure) is more cunning than submissive, and that he is really
preparing to escape to the freedom and independence of the
forest.[10]

Taken together these two works of art symbolize the psychological dimension of nationalism among French Canadians. The
'Last Huron' syndrome is the nightmare of ultimate extinction.
Légaré's deceptively submissive Indian represents the dream of
complete freedom. After nearly a century and a half, neither the
nightmare nor the dream has come true. But they remain part of
the French-Canadian nationalist psyche, as that psychiatrist
turned politician, Dr Camille Laurin, has often noted.[11]

Fear of the future, fear of extinction can be traced to at least two
sources. The first is historical. Defeat, something shared by Amer-
indians and *Canadiens,* is a central part of the French-Canadian
historical experience. In the beginning was the Conquest. Each
generation of French Canadians studies, reinterprets, and tries to
come to terms with this central fact of their history—and of all
Canadian history. Yet it never goes away. Here is a passage from
Dr Laurin's recent statement of policy on Quebec cultural development. It is a lengthy passage but it is a perfect summary of
the currently dominant view of the Conquest among Quebec
nationalists.

Then came the Conquest. A very small people, who had had, when all is said and done, a comparatively short time to take firm root in their territory, the 'anciens Canadiens' had to turn inwards on themselves and secure the foundations of their survival and growth in a country effectively taken over by another people, whose language, religion, law, political institutions, and character were alien to them. A conquered group, politically and economically subordinate, the 'Canadiens' little by little developed a minority mentality, and became increasingly marginal in a country where real power, though it was their own country, soon escaped them. Isolated, chiefly in the rural districts, they clung to their soil, their language, their religion, their customs of everyday life. The Conquest cut them off from participation in the mainstream of North American life and rendered them impervious, so to speak, to the great changes in the Western world: they settled down to 'endure', firmly anchored in the solid realities that are the stuff of peasant life.[12]

Each of the Parti Québécois's major public documents takes that sense of defeat symbolized by 1759 as its point of departure, once again demonstrating the centrality of the Conquest to nationalist thought.[13]

Consciousness of a second defeat has assumed an increasingly prominent place in the ideology of Quebec nationalism: the failure of Papineau's rebellion in 1837-8. In the past Papineau's anti-clerical side lessened his attraction for nationalist writers. But today, in a secular Quebec, he has been rehabilitated, and the *patriotes*, even though they failed, have gained a new respectability. 'A hundred and thirty years ago,' Robert-Lionel Séguin has written, 'the patiots of Saint-Denis showed us the way to dignity and freedom. A fertile seed whose fruits we are harvesting today.'[14]

To the Conquest and the abortive rebellion of 1837 other familiar defeats are often added: Riel's hanging, Manitoba schools, Regulation 17 in Ontario, conscription in two world wars, even the air-traffic-controllers' crisis of 1976 when the use of French in the air space over Quebec was prohibited. Victories, when they come, are always too late: the Supreme Court of Canada rejected restrictions on English in Quebec in less than three years after enactment; a Manitoba law abolishing French waited ninety years for the same result. A history filled with defeats and humiliations must surely stimulate pessimism. 'The only issue—a more or less long term issue,' a Montreal historian wrote in the 1950s, 'is the assimilation of the weaker culture by the stronger.' And yet that pessimistic nationalism was closely linked with the rise of separatism in the 1960s, and its historical interpretation is part of the official ideology of the Parti Québécois.[15]

Fear of the future has a second underlying cause: numbers. Throughout their history French Canadians have been preoccupied with their minority position. That is hardly surprising. New France was a tiny colony, outnumbered even by its Huron allies in the seventeenth century and constantly overshadowed by the more heavily populated English colonies to the south. While the French outnumbered the English in the Canadas until the 1850s, the pressure of English-speaking immigration was a major influence in the growth of the Parti Patriote in the 1830s.[16] One of the themes that run constantly through Garneau's *Histoire* is his fear for a future in which the *Canadiens* will be a minority. Again and again he refers to '*un peuple peu nombreux*', '*un peuple si faible en nombre*', and so on. 'But a small people,' he observed in explaining the French Canadians' attitude during the American Revolution, 'being unable to control its destiny, has to employ much caution and prudence.'[17]

Throughout the latter half of the nineteenth century French-Canadian leaders were extremely conscious of two demographic facts. The first was *la revanche des berceaux*. An extraordinarily high birth rate meant that French Canadians fulfilled the Malthusian law: population doubled every twenty-five years. 'During the last two centuries,' a Quebec demographer wrote in 1957, 'world population has been multiplied by three, European population by four, and French Canadian population by eighty, in spite of net emigration which can be estimated at roughly 800,000.'[18] Given those figures, even Sir John A. Macdonald's view that the solution to the French-Canadian problem lay in immigration and copulation sounds futile.

But the other half of the demographic picture for French Canadians was emigration, chiefly to the United States. That 'national hemorrhage' quite understandably obsessed French-Canadian leaders from the 1840s to the early twentieth century.[19] While some optimists thought that these southbound waves of Roman Catholics would one day restore puritan New England to the true faith,[20] the more frequent reaction was fear—fear that Quebec's population losses would be English Canada's political gain. Abbé J.-B.

Chartier put the issue very bluntly when he declared that only 'traitors' rejoiced at the sight of Quebeckers moving to the United States; keeping them at home was 'a question of life or death for the French-Canadian race.'[21] The campaigns of Curé Labelle, Arthur Buies, and others to colonize northern Quebec, and Canada, were conducted in the fulsome rhetoric of providential mission, but the goal was a very worldly one: to keep French Canadians at home where their heads could be counted by census-takers and vote-gatherers.

That preoccupation with numbers has not declined in the slightest. Nowhere in Canada is the decennial census scrutinized more thoroughly than in Quebec. In the last twenty-five years Quebec francophones have fully absorbed the values and aspirations of urban-industrial people everywhere. That has been accompanied by a dramatic decline in the birth rate. In 1961 Quebec's leading demographer, Jacques Henripin, speculated about population trends in Canada. If existing immigration and birth rates remained constant and French Canadians continued to adopt English at the 1961 rate, he predicted that by 1981 only 23.5 per cent of the Canadian population would be French-speaking, and that that percentage would fall to 17 by the year 2011. In 1951 the percentage was 29.[22] That statement, cautious and careful as it was, set off a chain reaction that led directly to Bill 101, the Charter of the French Language, in 1977. But before that stopping place had been reached the language issue had proven its potency: in Saint-Léonard something near communal strife erupted. Both the Union Nationale government of Jean-Jacques Bertrand and the Liberal administration of Robert Bourassa fumbled the issue. And that played a significant part in the election victory of the Parti Québécois in 1976. In the midst of these events a commission, known as the Gendron Commission, produced a massive report in which a convincing case was made for making French the working language of the province. Here was that Commission's conclusion:

This policy is in no sense an evasion of the problem of numbers. It is clear that both the reduction in the francophone birth rate and the inability of the French language to attract non-francophones are legitimate grounds for anxiety on the part of Franco-Quebeckers. The francophone fear of minority status, if it has little foundation within Quebec, obviously has much more reality in terms of Canada as a whole.[23]

'Fear of minority status': there is the heart of the matter. It is in fact the leit-motiv of much Quebec nationalist writing from Garneau through to successive policy statements of the Lévesque government. It was central to the White Paper on Language Policy, where one bold-face sub-heading summed up the issue: 'If the demographic evolution of Quebec continues, francophone Quebeckers will be increasingly fewer.' The same point is underlined in the opening pages of the cultural development policy statement and, inevitably, forms a central part of the argument for sovereignty-association. In the PQ government's White Paper *La Nouvelle Entente Québec-Canada* two large graphic illustrations provide the following information: in 1851, 36 per cent of Canadians were francophone; in 1971 that figure was 28 per cent, and by 2001 it will drop to 23 per cent. That in turn means that Quebec, which in 1867 held more than a third of the seats in the Canadian House of Commons, will by 2000 hold fewer than a quarter. 'Under these circumstances,' the authors of the White Paper argue, 'it would be an illusion to believe that, in future, francophones can play a determining role in the Government of Canada. On the contrary, they will be more and more a minority and English Canada will find it increasingly easy to govern without them. In that respect, far from being an anomaly, the Clark government is a sign of things to come.'[24]

By appealing to 'the fear of minority status', the Last Huron syndrome, the Lévesque government hopes to convince Quebeckers that the time has come to choose independence, to fulfil Joseph Légaré's vision of freedom. That theme, too, runs deeply in Quebec history. From the resort to arms in 1837 to Lévesque's proposed New Deal in 1979, the hope for independence has always remained alive among small groups of Quebeckers. For the most part it has never been much more than a dream to be achieved some day. After Papineau's defeat the dream of separate nationhood lived on in a segment of *le parti rouge* which opposed Confederation in 1865 (as did a few *bleus*, including the young Honoré Mercier). What the *rouges* favoured in 1865 was not complete independence but a loose form of federalism in which the member states would remain sovereign. When the Quebec Resolutions passed the Canadian Assembly (27 French Canadians in favour, 22 opposed), a newspaper of *rouge* persuasion fulminated: 'On that memorable night was committed the most contemptible, most degrading action the parliamentary system has witnessed since the treason of the Irish MPs who sold their country to England for places, honours, and gold.'[25]

Like much else in Quebec in the latter part of the nineteenth century, the idea of independence gradually acquired a clerical and conservative tone though its origins with the *rouges* had been secular and liberal.[26] Its chief exponent, Jules-Paul Tardivel (his enemies called him Jules-Paul Torquemada after the head of the Spanish Inquisition), edited a newspaper characteristically called *La Vérité*. In the 1880s, Riel's execution and Macdonald's centralizing policies convinced him that only independence would save Quebec from Anglo-Saxon Protestant domination. In his utopian novel, *Pour la patrie*, published in 1895, he described the events which, with God's help, led to independence in 1945. One passage, explaining the nationalist goal, is especially interesting:

Our geographical position, our natural resources and the homogeneity of our population enable us to aspire to be ranked among the nations of the earth. It is possible that Confederation offers certain material advantages, but from the religious and national point of view it is filled with dangers for us, for our enemies will certainly manage to wear it away until it is a legislative union in everything but name. Moreover the chief material advantages that are derived from Confederation could be obtained equally well through a simple postal and customs union.[27]

In addition to the obvious similarities to sovereignty-association as devised by the Parti Québécois, Tardivel's projected *République de la Nouvelle-France* contains some other revealing details. Most notable was the assumed peaceful manner of its achievement—no revolution, no civil war, just a rather heated parliamentary debate, in which a sympathetic English-Canadian Catholic played a crucial role. René Lévesque's plans are postulated on a similar assumption. Canadians, he believes, are sufficiently civilized to be able to work out a division of their country in a federal-provincial conference, presumably on prime-time television with suitable commentary.

Those who kept the light of Quebec independence alive during the generations that followed Tardivel were equally reasonable in their expectations. In 1922 Canon Lionel Groulx and his friends in *l'Action française* published an enquiry into *Notre Avenir politique* which concluded that the future was unfolding, as expected, towards independence. But it would come as a natural evolution 'as soon as Providence wishes it'.[28] French Canadians were called upon to prepare themselves, but the timetable was unspecified. So, too, the young separatists who joined with André Laurendeau in *Jeune Canada* in the late thirties spoke only in terms of an undefined future when, by undefined means, 'one day, a Country will be born.'[29]

Until the 1960s, then, when *Le Rassemblement pour l'indépendance nationale* and later the Parti Québécois were born, the ideal of independence was simply that, an ideal, more perhaps a state of mind than a concrete political project. Yet it is impossible not to be struck by the degree to which the Parti Québécois fits into this tradition of ambiguity and caution. Independence by stages: *étapisme*. Not even Mackenzie King, that Canadian master of ambiguity, of never doing things by halves that could be done by quarters, could have improved on the Révesque-Morin strategy. First the removal of the independence issue from the 1976 election by the promise of a referendum. Then a definition of independence that is not independence but sovereignty-association. Next a referendum asking not for approval of sovereignty-association, but merely a mandate to negotiate. Finally a promise of yet another referendum on the outcome of the negotiations. Everything is hedged. Is it any wonder that a muscular separatist like Pierre Vallières, in frustration, has pronounced the PQ strategy 'as ineffectual in liberating Quebec as the impromptu revolt of the Patriotes in 1837-8'?[30]

Why is nationalism in Quebec so cautious in tactics, so modest in its demands? Légaré's Indian may be preparing to escape into freedom, for the canoe lies ready. Yet he is also in the act of surrendering his bow to the statue of Wolfe. Perhaps it is not Mercury after all but rather, as the playwright Robert Gurik once contended, Hamlet who is *Prince du Québec*.[31] If, as I have been arguing, French-Canadian nationalism is driven by a fear of extinction, on the one hand, and the dreams of absolute freedom, on the other, then it is driven in contradictory directions. Fear of the future and hope for the future combine to create indecision, ambiguity, paradox. Is that not Papineau, brilliantly characterized by Fernand Ouellet as *Un Être divisé,* and by Garneau as *'l'image de notre nation'*? Caught between the desire to preserve and the desire to liberate, between nationalism and liberalism, he was paralysed, a Franklin without being a Washington.[32]

Garneau himself expressed that same tension which is at the heart of French-Canadian nationalism. At the conclusion of his great *Histoire,* having surveyed the struggles of his people from the first arrival of the explorers to the union of 1840, he drew one last lesson. It is often quoted, and rightly so, for it catches, as nothing else does, the essential character of nationalism in Quebec:

> Let the *Canadiens* be true to themselves; let them be prudent and persistent, and not allow themselves to be seduced for a moment by the glitter of social and political novelties! They are not strong enough to indulge themselves in this matter. It is for the great peoples to try out new theories: they have room to give themselves every liberty. As for us, our strength derives in part from our traditions; if we are to depart from them or alter them, let us do it gradually.[33]

That sense of prudence, that belief in the need to tread carefully and to be guided by past traditions, has continued to characterize French Canadians throughout their history. And it is against the background of modest, but persistent, nationalism that the goals of Quebeckers can best be understood, whether they are expressed in the demand for equality of linguistic rights, special powers for the province of Quebec, or sovereignty-association.

Put simply, the goal of French Canadians has always been security; the strategy for its achievement is the recognition of equality. For a self-conscious minority, both the goal and the means of achieving it are perfectly understandable. By definition a minority is potentially at the mercy of the majority. It lacks security. It must discover a way to maximize its position, to find a mechanism that will allow it to act as equal or near equal. Consciously, or otherwise, this has always been the strategy of French Canadians anxious to preserve their national distinctiveness. And that includes virtually all French Canadians; for, though they have often been divided on means, they have never been divided on ends.

What strategies are possible and available? Papineau tried one route: equality established through independence. That is the tradition of *d'égal à égal,* the Parti Québécois call to arms. But the lesson that many of Papineau's followers drew from the rebellion's failure was that equality would have to be achieved within a political system that they shared with other Canadians. Equality might never be perfect, but it would be attainable. That was the central message of L.-H. Lafontaine's Address to the Electors of Terrebonne in 1840. He demanded, and received, an equal share of the power within the Union: that was what the Rebellion Losses Bill demonstrated. But the primary symbol of his success was the repeal of the prohibition against the use of French that had been part of the original Union constitution. He practised what Canon Groulx admiringly called 'a national policy'[34] by convincing French Canadians to stand united behind him and thus maximize their strength. This is the strategy of 'French Power' practised by every successful French-Canadian federal politician since Cartier: by the concentation of the minority's votes in one party it becomes a near-equal.

It is not a perfect strategy and, since it has resulted in defeats as well as victories, critics have devised alternatives. The primary one, historically, might be called 'fortress Quebec'. It stands between 'French Power' and separation, taking something from each. It argues that since French Canadians will always be a minority in the federal system, they should concentrate their talents at the provincial level where they are a majority. Quebec, as the homeland of French Canadians, should thus be recognized as a province *pas comme les autres* with powers, at least in some areas, equal to those of the federal government or of all the other provinces combined. This strategy was practised in a limited manner by Mercier in the 1880s, and by Duplessis and Lesage in more recent times. The Report of the Tremblay Commission on Constitutional Problems in the late 1950s worked this theory out most completely. And variations on the theme of 'fortress Quebec'—though offering fortress status to other provinces, too—can be found in Claude Ryan's recent proposal for *A New Canadian Federation*.[35]

Underlying each of these strategies is a conception of French Canada and/or Quebec as a distinctive society, a nation in one of several senses, deserving equality with its partner, English Canada. That equality is seen as a necessary condition for the security that alone will banish the Last Huron syndrome.

Discovering the formula that will guarantee francophones security through equality has been the persistent quest of Quebeckers for nearly two centuries. The very vitality of francophone culture today is testimony, surely, to the degree of success that French Canadians have achieved. Neither Garneau's fears nor Légaré's hopes have been fulfilled. Both possibilities remain, and so does the riddle on the face of the French-speaking sphinx.

The ambiguity remains because it is an accurate reflection of the reality of Quebec society, its hopes and its fears. But it is more than that. It also reflects the shrewdness of a small, determined people who have discovered over the centuries that in the end survival depends on themselves, and that no single strategy is perfect. Where some see ambiguity as a sign of weakness—'cultural fatigue',[36] the brilliant novelist Hubert Aquin called it—others, and I think correctly, judge it more sympathetically. 'The frequent duality of the French Canadians' allegiance,' Michel Morin and Guy Bertrand conclude their dissection of the public philosophy of Quebec, 'according to whether they were electing a federal or a provincial government, bears sufficient witness to the natural intelligence of the people, that is of individuals anxious to guarantee their freedom and their rights, by setting the princes who rule them at odds with each other.'[37]

NOTES

1. Jean-Guy Pilon, 'Quebec and the French Fact', in Philip Stratford and Michael Thomas, eds, *Voices From Quebec* (Toronto, 1977), pp. 2-3.
2. François-Marc Gagnon, 'Borduas: Father of Quebec Separatism?', *Vanguard*, June-July 1977.
3. Michel Morin et Claude Bertrand, *Le Territoire imaginaire de la culture* (Montreal, 1979).
4. Maurice Pinard and Richard Hamilton, 'The Parti Québécois Comes to Power', *Canadian Journal of Political Science*, XI, 4 (December 1978), pp. 739-75.
5. Pierre Vadeboncoeur, *La Dernière Heure et la première* (Montreal, 1970), p. 7.
6. Pierre Drouilly, 'Le paradoxe québécois', *Le Devoir*, 14 février 1980, p. 5.
7. See, for example, Gilles Bourque et Anne Legaré, *Le Québec: la question nationale* (Paris, 1978); Henry Milner, *Politics in the New Quebec* (Toronto, 1978); and

Denis Monière, *Le Développement des idéologies au Québec* (Montreal, 1977).
8. Jacques Monet, *The Last Cannon Shot: A Study of French-Canadian Nationalism, 1837-1850* (Toronto, 1969), p. 25.
9. James Huston, ed., *Le Répertoire national* (Montreal, 1893), vol. 1.
10. François-Marc Gagnon, 'The Hidden Image of Early French Canadian Nationalism: A Parable', *Arts Canada*, December 1979 - January 1980, pp. 11-14.
11. Camille Laurin, *Ma Traversée du Québec* (Montreal, 1970), p. 85.
12. *La Politique québécoise du développement culturel* (Quebec, 1978), vol. 1, pp. 50-1.
13. *Québec-Canada: A New Deal* (Quebec, 1979), pp. 3-4.
14. Robert-Lionel Séguin, *La Victoire de Saint-Denis* (Montreal, 1964), p. 45: Marcel Rioux, *La Question du Québec* (Paris, 1969), pp. 70-1.
15. Michel Brunet, *Canadians et Canadiens*, (Montreal, 1954), p. 30. Maurice Séguin, *L'Idée de l'indépendance au Québec* (Montreal, 1968). See also Michael D. Beheils, 'Prelude to Quebec's "Quiet Revolution": The Re-emergence of Liberalism and the Rise of Neo-Nationalism, 1940-1960' (unpublished Ph.D. thesis, York University, 1978), vol. 1, pp. 130-91.
16. Fernand Ouellet, *Le Bas Canada 1791-1840* (Ottawa, 1976), p. 214ff.
17. F.-X. Garneau, *Histoire du Canada* (5th ed., Paris, 1920), vol. 2, p. 392; Philippe Reid, 'François-Xavier Garneau et l'infériorité numérique des Canadiens français', *Recherches Sociographiques*, XV, 1, pp. 31-9.
18. Jacques Henripin, 'From Acceptance of Nature to Control: The Demography of the French Canadians since the Seventeenth Century', *Canadian Journal of Economics and Political Science*, XXIII, 1 (February 1957), pp. 10-19.
19. Yolande Lavoie, *L'Émigration des Canadiens aux États-Unis avant 1930* (Montreal, 1972).
20. E. Hamon, *Les Canadiens-Français de la Nouvelle Angleterre* (Quebec, 1891) pp. 155-6.
21. Cited in Christian Morissonneau, *La Terre promise: le mythe du nord québécois* (Montreal, 1978), p. 78.
22. Jacques Henripin, 'Évolution de la composition ethnique et linguistique de la population canadienne', *Relations*, XX, première année, (août 1961), pp. 207-9.
23. *La Situation de la langue française au Québec*, I, *La Langue de travail* (Quebec, 1972), p. 301.
24. 'La Politique québécoise de la langue française', *Le Devoir*, 2 avril 1977, p. 7; *Québec-Canada: A New Deal*, pp. 29-30.
25. Cited in J.-P. Bernard, *Les Rouges* (Montreal, 1971), p. 265.
26. Fernard Ouellet, 'Nationalisme canadien-français et laicisme au XIXe siècle', *Recherches Sociographiques*, IV, 1, janvier-avril 1963, pp. 44-70.
27. Jules-Paul Tardivel, *For My Country*, trans. by Sheila Fischman (Toronto, 1975), p. 39.
28. *Notre Avenir politique* (Montreal, 1923), p. 29.
29. André Laurendeau, *Notre Nationalisme* (Montreal, 1935), p. 50.
30. Pierre Vallières, *Un Québec impossible* (Montreal, 1968), p. 71.
31. Robert Gurik, *Hamlet, prince du Québec* (Montreal, 1968).
32. Cited in Fernand Ouellet, *Louis-Joseph Papineau: un être divisé* (Ottawa, 1961), p. 22.

33. Garneau, *Histoire*, p. 33.
34. Lionel Groulx, 'Un Chef de trente trois ans', in *Notre Maître, le passé*, (Second series, Montreal, 1936), p. 150.
35. The Constitutional Committee of the Quebec Liberal Party, *A New Canadian Federation* (1980), p. 12.
36. Hubert Aquin, 'The Cultural Fatigue of French Canada', in Larry Shouldice, *Contemporary Quebec Criticism* (Toronto, 1979), pp. 55-82.
37. Morin et Bertrand, *Le Territoire*, pp. 154-5.

Louis Balthazar

QUEBEC AT THE HOUR OF CHOICE

Quebeckers will soon be confronted with a choice between two options. They will have to say either yes or no to the question put forward by their government: 'Do you agree to give the government of Quebec a mandate to negotiate the proposed agreement between Quebec and Canada [i.e. political sovereignty and economic association]?' Whatever the answer to that question, it will be a qualified one. For Quebeckers are invited to say 'yes' to a 'mandate to negotiate' an agreement, with a firm commitment from their government that 'any change in political status resulting from these negotiations will be submitted to the people through a referendum'. In other words, a 'yes' would not mean much more than a willingness to explore the possibilities of a new deal, as the real political change would be left to a further referendum. They are, on the other hand, invited to answer 'no' by the Liberal Party of Mr Claude Ryan with the formal assurance that a new Canadian federation will be negotiated as soon as that party gains power. In other words, the result of the referendum won't be 'yes' or 'no' but either 'yes but' or 'no but'.

This is no accident but a clear sign that, in many ways, the current polarization of the Quebec population between the Parti Québécois and the Parti Libéral, between the 'yes' and the 'no', between sovereignty and Confederation, is an artificial one. Quebeckers don't want to be prisoners of a dilemma as to whether or not they should secede from the rest of Canada, whether or not they are in favour of a Canadian federation. This is simply not the issue. The issue is that the government of Quebec has become, in the last twenty years, the national government of French-speaking

Quebeckers, and that the dynamics of this new situation require a profound change in the necessary and desirable relationship between Quebec and the rest of Canada.

This is why, even though I will be dealing here with the options facing Quebec at the time of a referendum which has divided Quebeckers into two camps, you will find me talking much more about a consensus than about the current political cleavages. Paradoxically enough, these cleavages have no sense at all if they are not seen in the perspective of a broad nationalist consensus that originated in the early 1960s. To understand that consensus, it is therefore necessary to go back to the beginning of the Quiet Revolution, some twenty years ago.

1. FRENCH CANADIANS BECOME QUÉBÉCOIS
After the death of Premier Maurice Duplessis, Quebec was badly in need of modernizing its social structures and its government. In June 1960 a new team was put into power in Quebec City under the slogan 'It's time for a change.' That slogan was not an empty one. The change really came about. The new government applied itself to taking its responsibilities in many sectors that had been abandoned before either to the Church or to economic laissez-faire or to the interventionist federal government. To implement new programs in the fields of social security, education, culture, and economics, the civil service was completely reshaped and considerably enlarged.

The immediate consequence of that profound change was a great strengthening of the Quebec government and a new importance attributed to political intervention. On the other hand, modernization made it more and more difficult, if not impossible, for the Church to continue to play its traditional role of leadership among the French Canadians. The government of Quebec spontaneously took over that leadership.

Modernization implied also that the old French-Canadian nationalism, aiming essentially at the survival of an ethnic minority in Canada, based on a great fidelity to tradition, could no longer subsist. French-Canadian society had become urbanized and the old parish structure had lost much of its social meaning. Modern means of communication, such as television, had enlarged the areas of belonging and made obsolete the old allegiances such as the family, the village, the parish, the region. They had also homogenized the population along linguistic lines. Quebec had become something other than a province: it was a French network of communication. The government naturally sought to control that network.

At the same time, French-speaking Quebeckers became conscious of being a majority in Quebec society while, in many respects, they continued to be treated as a minority, especially in their largest metropolitan centre, Montreal, where anglophones controlled the major economic activities. In realizing this, they rediscovered nationalism in a new form. They were not content to survive; they wanted to enter the modern era and actually take over control of the society in which they were the majority.

All this led the government of Quebec to consider itself the holder of a very special responsibility: that of ensuring the development of a distinct culture in North America. When Mr Jean Lesage declared that Quebec had become the 'political expression of French Canada' and that it needed all the instruments to play that role, he was proclaiming the aspiration of his government to become a national government within the Canadian entity. As most French-speaking Quebeckers, more or less consciously, acquiesced in this new role for their government, they naturally ceased to identify themselves as French Canadians—which implied being a minority in Canada—and referred to themselves as Québécois.

This new phenomenon had two immediate obvious consequences. Since not all French Canadians were Quebeckers and not all Quebeckers were French Canadians, two groups of people were bound to be greatly disturbed by the new assertion.

First, the French Canadians living outside Quebec had the feeling of being left alone, since they could not share the new nationalism. Actually, Quebeckers had never taken the decision to abandon their fellow French Canadians in other provinces. It was much more a matter of a new reality that was imposing itself: the necessity for a modern culture to rest on a large network of communications for its development. Since the small areas, such as the village, the parish, the region, had lost their meaning, only a larger society could become a focus of allegiance. Only in Quebec could a modern French network of communications really exist.

Only in Quebec was it possible to aspire to build a really French society, to live in French on a daily basis in all walks of life. So the fact was not that the French minorities outside Quebec were abandoned, but rather that *their objects and those of the French-speaking Quebeckers were becoming completely different*. The latter wanted to build a new society to fit their culture; the former wanted to preserve some of their institutions in a society that would always inevitably remain English-speaking.

The second disturbing consequence was that, if French-speaking Quebeckers became a majority, the million or so of those who were English-speaking would become a minority. Here the change was to be even more abrupt and shocking. For the Quebec anglophones, far from considering themselves a minority, had for a long time seen themselves as the first Canadians, the pioneers of Canadian development, the proud inhabitants, most of them, of the metropolis of Canada. It is no wonder that their ears remained deaf to the new expressions of Quebec nationalism. It took them at least ten years to realize the painful necessity of adjusting to the reality of living in a francophone society. Since most of them had not even bothered to learn French, let alone to integrate into Quebec society, they had to be confronted with the serious demands of a linguistic law to decide either to adjust (as francophone minorities had always done outside Quebec) or to leave.

That is the essential dimension of Quebec nationalism: the ideal of a French Quebec with an English Canada (which does not mean that minorities in either society had to be wiped out, just that they had to accept the simple fact that Quebec is basically French, the rest of Canada basically English). That ideal has inspired the various claims of all Quebec governments since 1960, whether you call it 'special status' for Quebec or strong autonomy, a two-nation concept, cultural sovereignty, or even sovereignty-association. That ideal has met with a large consensus among the Quebec population. Not a single Quebec political party has ever declined to endorse it.

2. OTTAWA'S RESPONSE

The federal government in Ottawa, which had been modernizing for about twenty-five years before Quebec woke up, and had consequently strengthened its power over all Canada and the provincial governments, never really addressed itself to the new Quebec demands. As the Quebec government claimed responsibility for the development of a modern francophone society, Ottawa tried to devise plans that would allow French Canadians to feel at home in all of Canada. The idea of a country with two geographically identifiable linguistic areas has remained to this day heretical in Ottawa. Such an idea, it was said, would inevitably lead to the break-up of Canada. To avoid separatism, only one way was seen to be efficient, the progressive homogenization of all Canadians. To that end, instead of recognizing the French character of Quebec society, Ottawa policy-makers proceeded to encourage and emphasize, sometimes quite artificially, the use of the French language outside Quebec. The French radio and television networks were extended, delegates of other provincial governments were sent abroad to participate in international meetings of francophone countries, and large segments of the Ottawa bureaucracy were devoted to the reinforcement of French-Canadian culture so that Canadian bilingualism would appear to be truly horizontal, not vertical.

If some of these programs were welcomed by the French minorities outside Quebec, for so many years victims of gross violation of their basic rights, the profound difference between the claims of those minorities and the goals of Quebec was almost totally ignored.

However, the Royal Commission set up in 1963 to study the implications of bilingualism and biculturalism across Canada produced a preliminary report that came very close to recognizing the essential reality of the geographical linguistic cleavage. It put forward the concept of the two majorities; that is, for a modern culture to develop, it has to rely on the existence of a majority of people somewhere living according to that culture. In other words, the report stressed the obvious fact that the future of a French culture in Canada rested on a Quebec majority. This was an implicit recognition of the difference between the claims of francophones in Quebec and those of French minorities outside.

But that statement never became policy. The Commission later de-emphasized the idea of biculturalism to promote the concept of multiculturalism, and thus encouraged an enduring confusion between minority culture (or ethnic culture) and global culture.

Between a single Canadian culture and several ethnic sub-cultures, there was no room for the francophone culture of Quebec and its claim to mould a whole society. Moreover, as Mr P.E. Trudeau came to power in 1968, all the report's ideas were dropped for the sake of one major goal of the Liberal government: the promotion of bilingualism throughout Canada.

Nobody was really satisfied by bilingualism. For a French Canadian, to see signs in both languages in federal government buildings in Vancouver, while obviously British Columbia remained an anglophone society, was of little comfort. At the same time, the city of Montreal was still a place where it was often difficult to speak French and where immigrants spontaneously adopted the English language. The Quebec government's aspiration to be endowed with all the powers it needed to be the national government of a francophone society was still blunted. And anglophone Canadians were often bemused if not irritated by all those French signs within their own very English territories.

By 1976, nothing was really solved. So, after a so-called separatist government was elected in Quebec, a new task force was set up to look for the means of preserving Canadian unity. Again, the federally appointed commission came out with a very lucid assessment of the reality. It declared, among other things, that one of the fundamental problems of Canada lay in its *duality* (the other being regionalism). Quebec, the report continued, has to be recognized as the francophone cultural metropolis in North America (whether or not it stays in the Canadian Confederation). Quebec represents a specific society within Canada, owing to its own history, language, civil law, the common origins of its population, feelings, politics, etc. And finally, the report goes on to define duality as the relation between Quebec and the rest of Canada.

Like the 'B and B' Report, the Pépin-Robarts Report was quickly shelved after the usual official greeting. In the two federal elections that followed its publication, it was conspicuously ignored by all federal political parties. Paradoxically, the best reception it ever got came from the 'separatist' government of Quebec. This of course left Quebeckers completely disenchanted with the federal attitude towards them. Actually many of them had known disenchantment a long time before.

Back in 1968, when Prime Minister Trudeau proceeded to put an end to Quebec efforts to obtain special status or at least more power in order to meet its special responsibilities, quite a few political leaders resorted to a new formula to attain the basic goals of the Quebec people. Under the leadership of the former Liberal minister René Lévesque, the 'Mouvement Souveraineté-Association', launched in the fall of 1967, gave birth to a new party, the Parti Québécois, which was to polarize Quebec political life along constitutional lines to the present day.

3. THE MEANING OF THE PQ

This new party has appeared to most people as the party of those who want the separation of Quebec from Canada, or, if you put it more positively, the party of those who want political independence for Quebec. Such an appearance does not, in my opinion, adequately correspond to reality.

When René Lévesque left the Quebec Liberal Party, after trying unsuccessfully to carry a strong nationalist platform through its 1967 convention, he laid the basis of a movement that would call for the sovereignty of Quebec coupled with a tight economic association with Canada. Lévesque is undoubtedly a Quebec nationalist for whom the Quebec identity is paramount above any other consideration. But, in a sense, he is also a Canadian. At least, some form of Canadian union has a meaning for him. Separatism has always appeared to him as something ugly and anachronistic. A modern nation, in his eyes, cannot afford to be separated from larger ensembles. One might even say he is a federalist at heart.

What brought him to call for sovereignty-association was an interpretation of the 1960s struggle for a new status for Quebec. For him, the Canadian government, under the Confederation scheme, was and would remain essentially centralist and unitarian. It would tolerate provincial governments as some form of regional authority but could never delegate to Quebec the amount of power needed for the development of a genuine and distinct society. That interpretation, for better or for worse, led him to the ideal of sovereignty; but he could never resign himself to sacrifice the Canadian union completely. In fact, he was still dreaming of a special status for Quebec in the framework of a new confederation (in the real sense of that word).

Of course, all the separatists of Quebec were attracted by his leadership and gathered around him, and the few Liberals who had defected with him, to form the new Parti Québécois. The majority of the new party's members were former adherents of the RIN (Rassemblement pour l'Indépendance Nationale). This inevitably gave the party a very separatist outlook. The idea of association was quickly relegated to a secondary status and most of the party faithful were carrying high the banner of sovereignty.

The PQ was easily defeated by the Liberals at the 1970 election, but it had seven members elected to the National Assembly with an impressive twenty-three per cent of the popular vote. In 1973, it became the official opposition with thirty per cent of the vote, although it did poorly in the election of members with only six elected. The PQ, because of the Lévesque charisma, a progressive platform, and a solid and democratic organization, became very attractive to Quebec youth and to all those who sought a valid alternative to an increasingly arrogant and corrupt Liberal Party. But at the same time, to become acceptable to a majority of French-speaking Quebeckers, it had to drop its radical separatist outlook. The idea of complete independence for Quebec was never approved by much more than fifteen per cent of the population; so when in 1976 forty-one per cent of Quebeckers gave their support to the PQ many of them did so because they felt protected by a firm PQ commitment not to declare independence unilaterally and to submit the formula of sovereignty-association to a referendum.

It is worth noting that none of the names that had been associated previously with hard-core separatism (Raymond Barbeau, Marcel Chaput, André d'Allemagne, Pierre Bourgault) were among the PQ majority returned to the Assembly in 1976. On the other hand, one could see in the new cabinet many people who had been involved, one way or another, in the struggle of the 1960s for a stronger Quebec within Confederation: Claude Morin (a deputy minister under the four previous Quebec premiers), Jacques Parizeau, Jacques-Yvan Morin, and others.

Moreover, the PQ has emphasized more and more the idea of association with the rest of Canada, so much so that the party rank and file became irritated with what they interpreted as a betrayal of the ideal of independence. They had forgotten that association had been coupled with sovereignty at the very beginning of their party. Some might say, as was said frequently in the anglophone press in

Canada, that this soft language was hypocritical and was intended only to make the hesitant Quebec population swallow the pill of independence more easily. It seems to me more valid to say that PQ leaders were simply recognizing the Quebec consensus as it is: a better status for Quebec within the framework of a necessary and desirable Canadian union.

So the PQ may be less separatist than was thought. One might also say that the Liberal Party, under the leadership of committed federalists such as Robert Bourassa and Claude Ryan, is much more nationalist than it is usually assumed to be.

The Bourassa government, in spite of its very federalist and anti-separatist outlook, was responsible for the abortion of the Victoria federal-provincial constitutional conference in 1971. The Canadian constitution was not patriated from Great Britain because of Premier Bourassa's firm demands in the field of social security. It was also his government that waged a tough fight on jurisdiction over communications. It came out with linguistic legislation (Bill 22) that infuriated the leaders of the anglophone population of Quebec, perhaps more than the later PQ Charter of the French Language. Its call for 'cultural sovereignty' provoked Ottawa's anger, ambiguous as it may have appeared to many in Quebec.

As for Claude Ryan, the new leader, he has in the past, as publisher and editorialist of *Le Devoir*, always espoused the cause of stronger powers for the Quebec government, and has taken enough nationalist stances to make one believe that his recent rage against PQ nationalism is inspired more by his partisan position than by any profound conviction.

So it seems that the two main political parties of Quebec are steadily drawing closer to the centre of the spectrum, from their original antagonistic posture. I don't want to deny the major differences between the Liberal and PQ alternatives. Those differences remain very important. But one should never forget that it would not take much of a blunder on the part of the federal government to make the two parties side with each other. Jean Chrétien, when he was minister of finance, found this out when his sales-tax rebate policy was rejected unanimously by the Quebec National Assembly.

But undeniably the Quebec consensus will be less and less

apparent in the months to come. The referendum issue will make Quebeckers fight fiercely against one another. For the voters will have to choose definitely between two conceptions of a better future for Quebec.

4. SOVEREIGNTY-ASSOCIATION: THE NEW DEAL

In the fall of 1979, the PQ government tabled its White Paper on sovereignty-association. The paper begins with a broad and selective historical review, taking short cuts to prove its main point: that French Canadians have been constantly lured by their English masters. It goes on to depict the experience of Canadian federation as a negative one for Quebec, leading to an irremediable deadlock. In the discussion of the two federal commissions mentioned above, the conclusion is drawn by the PQ government that 'to solve the Quebec-Canada political problem . . . a different formula must be found.'

That formula is political sovereignty for Quebec in matters of lawmaking, taxation, and external relations, and economic association with the rest of Canada. The association proposed is the closest possible, that is to say a monetary union which would imply the free circulation of goods and people between Quebec and the new Canada.

To administer that union, four agencies are suggested: a community council, a commission of experts, a court of justice, and a monetary authority. All four would be composed of members appointed by the two sovereign governments. A community parliament is not foreseen. Here lies probaby the main weakness of the proposal. At a time when European countries, though far from being involved in a union as tight as the one proposed by the PQ, accept the idea of an elected European parliament, it is difficult to see why Quebeckers and Canadians would not want to set up a democratic institution to administer their close union.

The PQ government doesn't seem, from the White Paper, to have foreseen all the implications of a monetary union. That union would inevitably entail a common economic policy. Why would that policy be left to representatives of two sovereign governments? Isn't economic policy one of the most vital political issues these days? Moreover, I do not see how a common economic policy could fail to lead to common foreign policies in many international issues. And why not a common defence policy?

The White Paper remains silent on those questions, maybe because it does not want to have to admit the blunt fact that a type of association like the one proposed imposes severe constraints on the political independence so dear to the most ardent members of the PQ.

But the paper argues well against one of the major objections made to the proposal: that most responsible politicians in English Canada have bluntly rejected the idea of negotiating association with Quebec even if Quebeckers should pronounce in favour of such negotiations:

> Stating that there will be no economic association is tantamount to saying that English Canada is ready to get along without the Quebec market, that it will create its own separate currency to avoid sharing one with Quebec. And that the Maritimes will agree to have a customs barrier put up between them and Ontario! It would then be the rest of Canada that would reject the advantages of economic union.

In any case, it is hard to think that those who today advocate preserving Canadian unity would willingly provoke the complete balkanization of Canada for the sake of not negotiating with Quebec.

Moreover, in the referendum question the Quebec government is asking the population for a mandate to negotiate and is committed to return to the people to have them endorse a political change. What does it mean? Quite possibly, although the PQ government would not admit it, it may mean what is implied in any negotiation, that the negotiator is willing to accept a result that would fall short of his original proposal. Is it impossible to conceive that somewhere in between the ideal of sovereignty-association and the present Confederation lies the sort of renewed federalism that the Quebec population would be willing to endorse?

On the other hand, the threat put forward by many federal politicians against the eventuality of a 'yes' answer by a majority of the Quebec voters, i.e. that there would be no negotiation at all, is not a valid one. How would the Quebec population react to such a rejection of their will? Chances are that their pride would make them react drastically, although it is neither in their nature nor in their interest to do so, and bring them closer to supporting a unilateral declaration of independence.

At any rate, Prime Minister Clark's reaction has seemed so far the most civilized one: 'Yes or no, I'll be there to negotiate.' It is hard to think that English Canadians' interests would be foresaken by their representatives sitting to negotiate a new arrangement with Quebec.

5. THE RYAN ALTERNATIVE

But the Quebec population may say 'no' to the referendum question. Not that it is willing to say 'no' to change, but it may see better chances of bringing about a renewed federalism in refusing the PQ's new deal and later electing the Liberal Party to the government of Quebec. The Liberal Party's Constitutional Committee has recently produced its own proposal for a new Confederation called the Beige Paper. What's in it for the achievement of the fundamental Quebec aspiration to greater autonomy?

The Liberal paper is well within the Quebec tradition when it emphasizes the distinct character of the French province: 'Within the Canadian political family, Quebec society has all the characteristics of a distinct national community.' Although it does not claim a special status for Quebec, it proposes serious changes in the partition of power between the federal and the provincial governments that would certainly give more power to the Quebec government.

Its boldest proposition concerns the creation of a Federal Council to replace our obsolete Senate. The new institution would be composed of delegates from the various provinces, and its role would be to check the power of the federal government in constitutional matters and to advise it from a provincial point of view. A permanent 'dualist' committee of the Council would be created to reflect the fundamental character of the federation in cultural and linguistic matters. This committee would ratify any federal action in those matters.

All those changes, however, as radical as they may be, still fall short of many ardent Quebec claims of the past twenty years. And it does not seem to be concerned as much with Quebec's place in the Canadian Confederation as with the renewal of the constitution as a whole. As such, it might as well come from a federal institution as from a Quebec political party. There may be some nobility of mind in that detachment from Quebec concerns, but it is not likely to reflect the aspirations of Quebec as they have been expressed by our various governments since 1960.

Furthermore, what looked like changes in the division of powers between levels of government are actually more clarifications and limitations of federal power, rather than real decentralization and increase of provincial powers, except for the transfer of residual powers from Ottawa to the provinces.

The Beige Paper may even be considered a step backward compared with former Quebec claims in fields as important as taxation (where greater fiscal responsibility was demanded), social policies (where Quebec claimed full jurisdiction), and communications (where the document is more timid than the Bourassa government).

But the big question remains: how is it going to be implemented? Even though the Liberal paper has had an obviously better reception in English Canada than the PQ one, the same objection can be made to it as to sovereignty-association. What if the partners refuse? The partners so far have expressed their willingness to discuss and negotiate. But what is going to be left of the bold proposals after negotiation? If the PQ proposal goes too far, one can at least envisage a reduced version of it as progress for Quebec. What progress would be left after each Canadian province and the federal government had produced their amendments to the Liberal formula?

Those are questions to which the answers are hardly more reassuring than those given to the PQ riddle. The paradox is that, as *Le Devoir*'s editor-in-chief, Michel Roy, has put it, implementation of the Liberal proposal may well depend on a 'yes' vote in the referendum. Such a vote would surely produce enough pressure on English Canadians to give Mr Ryan, if and when elected, the authority to extort concessions to his claims. Quite an embarrassing situation for the leader of the 'No' campaign in the referendum!

So far, Mr Ryan has scored strong points over Mr Lévesque in their contest. It may be that Quebeckers are ready to entrust the former rather than the latter with the mission of bringing about the desired changes in the Canadian constitution. But the Liberal

Party's Constitutional Committee's paper seems unlikely to be of great assistance to Mr Ryan in the contest. It would be surprising if Quebeckers became very enthusiastic over it.

But whatever the choice of the Quebec population is, let us never forget that it will be qualified, very qualified indeed. For unfortunately the Quebec consensus may lie in between the 'yes' and the 'no'. If it were possible, Quebeckers might just answer 'Yeah'!

EPILOGUE: AFTER THE REFERENDUM

On 20 May 1980 a strong majority of Quebeckers refused to give their government a mandate to negotiate sovereignty-association. Many of them, while still treasuring their Quebec identity, were persuaded that a 'yes' vote had to be identified with the separation of Quebec from the rest of Canada, so they voted for the maintenance of their Canadian connection. During the campaign they were constantly reminded that their commitment to Canada would in no way affect their primary allegiance to Quebec. Indeed the slogan of the 'No' forces was 'Mon non est québécois'. Paradoxically, people had to be brought to vote for Canada in the name of Quebec.

This should be sufficient to demonstrate that the 'no' vote was indeed very qualified. Unfortunately that qualification did not appear on the ballots and in the official results. Many Canadians, therefore, interpreted the 'No' victory as an unconditional commitment of the Quebeckers to the Canadian Confederation. First and foremost among them was Prime Minister Trudeau, who proposed, three weeks after the referendum, a preamble to a new Constitution that ignored totally the contention of French-speaking Quebeckers that they are a distinct people. For him, obviously, the 'no' was not Québécois but simply Canadian.

Already it is clear that Mr Ryan is no more receptive than Mr Lévesque to the first proposals for a new constitution that have come from Ottawa. But it will not be easy for two parties (one of which is composed of militants who are not too keen on constitutional talks) to agree on a common position as they prepare to wage a tough fight in the forthcoming provincial election.

However, there *is* a common consensus among provincial politicians in Quebec; namely, that two major principles must be recognized in a new Canadian constitution: (i) the existence of two founding peoples in Canada; and (ii) the right of Quebec to self-determination. The second of these two principles was already recognized in fact by the exercise of the referendum and by the legal existence of a separatist movement in Quebec. However, it will be extremely difficult to embody such a principle in the Canadian constitution, if only because by its very nature it emphasizes what holds a country together; it does not concern itself with anything that may eventually bring about its dissolution. Nevertheless the right of self-determination could be admitted implicitly by stressing the freedom of the social contract and by recognizing that the federation is formed by joining together social units, not individuals; this is true of any federation.

The existence of two founding peoples should be recognized in order to satisfy a majority of Quebeckers. However, the word 'founding' should be dropped from this principle and the word 'two' changed. 'Founding peoples' has an undesirable ethnic connotation. If Quebeckers can claim to be a people, it is because for the most part they are one today, which is a fact based on sociological evidence—not because one day in history their ancestors founded a society. Many 'founding peoples' have disappeared. And neither the French nor the English pioneers were the first to occupy this North American land. The Indians and Eskimos were founders too, in some respects. Moreover, English Canada has obviously become something quite different from the British society first established by the Loyalists and others. It has become a mosaic of peoples from several ethnic backgrounds, all equal to one another and all united by a common culture and a common language. But Quebeckers, for their part—and this cannot be emphasized enough—can no longer be considered an ethnic group. Quebec of its own is, and will become more and more, an identifiable and distinct society whose people are united by the French language and an evolving Quebec culture.

This is the essential point about Quebec: that it constitutes a distinct people and that Quebec's government should be granted all the powers necessary to preside over the destiny of that people. Its partner in Confederation may be one English Canada or a number of autonomous regions (e.g. British Columbia, the Prairies, Ontario, and the Maritimes); but whatever the arrangement, the fundamental claim of Quebec to being recognized as a specific francophone society will not change. Notwithstanding the 'no' answer to the referendum, Canada will have to live with that claim for years to come.

Many observers have seen in Quebec nationalism a pheno-menon of ethnocentrism. Spokesmen for that nationalism have often given ground for such a view, but the main trend of the new Quebec dynamism is not and cannot be in that direction. Quebec is a territory, a culture, a network of communications. It cannot be an ethnic entity. One million non-French-speaking people live in Quebec. They will gradually become more and more integrated into the society and so will accept French as the main language of communication, though they will not assimilate totally and a great number of them will continue to make limited use of the English language. So far a majority of them have been reluctant to integrate (as has been the case in English Canada with ethnic minorities there, including the French). But a growing number of them are becoming authentic Quebeckers and, more importantly, all the children from different ethnic backgrounds who now attend French schools in Quebec—the Quebeckers of tomorrow—are already constituting the new Quebec mosaic.

Surely French-speaking Quebeckers will have to change their thinking. They will have to learn not to look upon themselves as a homogeneous ethnic group (calling themselves French Canadi-ans) and to welcome other ethnic groups into their culture, much as the United States and English Canada have done. On that transformation depends the future of the new concept of Quebec.

The future of Canada, on the other hand, depends on the recog-nition of that concept of Quebec by all Canadians, as well as on the wording of a new Canadian constitution.

III
The Economy and the State

Michael Bliss

'RICH BY NATURE, POOR BY POLICY': THE STATE AND ECONOMIC LIFE IN CANADA

The relationship that ought to prevail between the state and the private sector is bound to be an important issue on the agenda of Canadian public debate in the 1980s. The only way a historian can properly participate in a debate about the future is by looking backwards. This essay is an exploration of the historical relationship between the public and private sectors in Canada, organized around reflections on a comment that a Canadian intellectual, Goldwin Smith, made in 1891. '"Rich by nature, poor by policy" might be written over Canada's door,' Smith wrote in his pessimistic book, *Canada and the Canadian Question*.[1]

The comment was an attack on Canada's protective tariff. This policy of protection for Canadian industries was called the National Policy and was the most visible, dramatic, and influential use of state power to mould the Canadian economy attempted in the nineteenth century. The argument of this essay is twofold and partly schizophrenic: first, that Goldwin Smith may have been right in his belief that government action tended to make Canadians poorer than nature intended; second, that it did not matter very much whether or not Goldwin Smith was right, because he and the views he championed were impractical and irrelevant. No matter how badly it worked, Canadians were determined to use the force of government to attempt to make themselves rich by policy. This determination, this addiction to big government, is as likely to prevail in the 1980s as it did in the 1880s.

The one non-contentious statement that can be made about government involvement in Canadian economic life is that we have had a lot of it. Twenty years ago the economic historian H.G.J. Aitken published what has become a classic article, 'Defensive Expansion: The State and Economic Growth in Canada', in which he wrote,

> The standard interpretation of the entire history of the Canadian economy assigns to the state a major role in guiding and stimulating development: on any reading of the historical record, government policies and decisions stand out as the key factors. The creation of a national economy in Canada and, even more clearly, of a transcontinental economy was as much a political as an economic achievement.[2]

Far from disputing Aitken's claim that government has played a more active role in shaping the economy in Canada than it has in the United States, Canadian historians and political philosophers have stressed this activity as a key to the differences between Canadian and American political cultures. At the extreme we find Herschel Hardin arguing in his not uninfluential book, *A Nation Unaware*, that the 'public enterprise culture' of Canada is the key to the Canadian identity, potentially the unique contribution Canadians have to make to world culture.[3] Supposing then that the Aitken-to-Hardin line of argument about the *extent* of state activity in Canada is correct,[4] we should not assume that the last word has been written on the beneficial *effect* of that activity. An interesting body of recent Canadian historiography suggests that important new questions are being asked about the consequences of the economic acts of past Canadian governments.

For two generations after about 1920 Canadians gradually forgot how contentious the National Policy of tariff protection had actually been. As the nation and its economy matured, as the tariff disappeared as a political issue in Canada, our historical memory stressed how well the National Policy seemed to have worked during the great boom around the turn of the century. The tariff, along with the state-supported transcontinental railway and the policies of Western development, took on the aura of key ingredients in a kind of recipe of Canadian national development, ingredients which all blended together in memory as one national policy and were seen to have been generally necessary, effective, and, consequently, good. Sour comments by out-of-date—in fact dead—Victorian liberals such as Goldwin Smith were forgotten about, as were charges by the old Liberal opponents of the National Policy that it ranged from 'legalized robbery' all the way to 'socialism'.[5]

Economists, however, did not forget their theoretical objections to tariffs, and Canadian historians were forcefully reminded of these in the mid-1960s when the economic historian John Dales published his powerful critique of the National Policy tariff as resulting in an unnecessary reduction in the per-capita incomes of Canadians.[6] Dales's attack on the National Policy has not only not been seriously challenged since its publication, but has in fact been supplemented by a cluster of other concerns about the impact of the tariff, ranging from nationalists' dislike of its apparent branch-plant-inducing effects to the implicit beliefs of confused Marxists that it was an impediment to the development of Canadian manufacturing.[7] It is perhaps a measure of how little real enthusiasm there still is for the historic National Policy that so little attention was paid to its centenary in 1979. In the one published *Festschrift* to the National Policy, the Fall 1979 issue of the *Journal of Canadian Studies*, the ambivalence of the several authors who attempt to measure the effects of that tariff is striking.[8]

A similar ambivalence, tending towards a critical reappraisal, has developed regarding the other national development policies pursued in the late nineteenth century. For many historians, for example, the most interesting contribution to Canadian historiography resulting from the publication of Pierre Berton's history of the building of the CPR was a review of his first volume by H.V. Nelles. In a minor *tour de force*, Nelles argued that the Macdonald-Creighton-Berton 'Railroad Now' approach to the building of the CPR is vulnerable in half-a-dozen important premises. Writing of the unlikelihood of a serious American threat to the Canadian West, the unimpressive claims about the need for the line north of Superior, and the likelihood that the CPR was built ten years or so before it was needed, among other factors, Nelles concluded by asking, 'Did the country pay too high a price for the transcontinental railway?'[9] Yes, the economic historian Peter George was already answering, having applied quantitative methods to the construction of the CPR to show that it was apparently built prematurely and at excessive cost.[10]

George's work in the late 1960s foreshadowed the emergence of a new group of Canadian economic historians, well versed in both economic theory and the techniques of quantification, who are now beginning to have a major impact on our view of economic development in the late nineteenth century. Much of their work hinges on asking questions about the impact of federal government policy on the settlement of Western Canada. Their conclusions, as summarized by Kenneth Norrie, who is himself one of the most important of these new economic historians, make virtually every Canadian history textbook and probably most lectures in Canadian history seem grossly out of date:

The link between the occurrence of the wheat boom and the national policy [in its tripartite sense], made often and casually in the past, seems to have been rejected, but so has the rote recitation of a series of external disturbances. The emphasis has shifted instead to a more carefully specified series of exogenous factors, specifically the end of the U.S. frontier of sub-humid land, the development and diffusion of appropriate dry farming techniques, and the movements in relative real wages in Canada, the U.S. and the U.K. Within this view the federal government's promotional efforts played a role only insofar as they aided in the development and diffusion of dry farming technology, increased the speed by which settlers reacted to the emergent profit possibilities through advertising expenditures, and aided in the development of branch lines. In all these cases, though, it still needs to be established that the national policy did not simply substitute for developments that would have occurred anyway. In addition, for the policy to be judged a success in even these modest dimensions, it must be true that the resulting additions to the total output exceeded the opportunity costs of the resources used in promoting them. . . .

Recent contributions . . . have questioned whether even this is a sufficient evaluation of these development strategies. They argue instead that the very institutional structures of the free homestead and railway land grant systems probably induced agricultural settlement and rail line construction before it was socially profitable. In other words, far from being beneficially stimulative or even largely irrelevant, the policies actually led to a significant misallocation of scarce resources.[11]

Conclusions like these seem to vindicate some of the nineteenth-century liberal critics of Canada's national development policies.

While the reconsideration of national policies is the most visible and interesting area in which questions are being asked about the impact of the state on the Canadian economy, other aspects of government involvement in enterprise are also coming under historians' scrutiny. There used to be a popular view of railway development in the Laurier period, for example, comparing William Mackenzie and Donald Mann to the Duke and Dauphin in *Huckleberry Finn* as they literally took the Canadian public for a ride on their privately owned and privately looted and unnecessary Canadian Northern Railway.[12] It was not widely noticed that the official historian of the CNR, G.R. Stevens, actually found the Canadian Northern to be a well-constructed, honestly financed, nearly viable railway system, and instead considered the Laurier government's politically planned and semi-state-owned Grand Trunk Pacific/National Transcontinental system to have involved a near-criminal misuse of public funds.[13] The publication in 1976 of T.D. Regehr's definitive history of the Canadian Northern completed the rehabilitation of this Mackenzie and Mann project. The implications of Regehr's book went further: in his demonstration of how Mackenzie and Mann had attempted to build railroads in the new environment of state regulation of rates and profits, and how erratic, nearly irrational behaviour by regulatory bodies had shattered their assumptions, Regehr made the first recent contribution to the discussion in Canada of an issue of great concern to American economic historians: the impact of government regulation on industries. It will not be surprising if someone follows Regehr's lead on this issue and reaches conclusions similar to Albro Martin's about American railways, that regulation was a major reason for the decline of the industry.[14]

The only thorough study we have of provincial development policies and their impact is H.V. Nelles's widely acclaimed work on Ontario's resource policies in the century before World War II, *The Politics of Development*. Nelles's conclusions about Ontario's policies—that they contributed to the reduction of the state to 'a client of the business community' and did not result in bringing the 'business and technical functions of the state' into the 'realm of democratic accountability'—has been used by scholars on the left as evidence of the way in which the 'positive state' in Canada often becomes state capitalism in the interests of powerful groups in the private sector.[15] This, of course, is true. But more important for the purposes of this paper is the fact of Nelles's demonstration that Ontario's development policies did not work effectively. As the state expanded its activities in response to the pressures of interested groups, there was a misallocation of resources. Although Nelles would not concur, it can be argued that his diagnosis leads as readily to a prescription of less government involvement in development, less behaviour as a 'client' of interest groups, and more holding of enterprises accountable through arm's-length dealing, as it does to the notion that the remedy for government incompetence is more government activity.

The most striking aspect of Nelles's book is his detailed, critical account of the operations of Ontario Hydro, North America's first publicly owned electrical company. For the people of Ontario a major consequence of public ownership of hydro was to enable Sir Adam Beck to create a ruthless, irresponsible monopoly, of doubtful competence, freed from the discipline of either the marketplace or informed legislators. 'In the name of the people,' Nelles writes of Ontario Hydro at the peak of its early expansion in 1919, 'the Hydro-Electric Power Commission was literally running away with the provincial treasury, and no one had the courage to ask for what purpose.'[16] In this first study by a trained historian of one of Canada's showpiece public enterprises, the public enterprise does not receive particularly high marks. There is a tendency in Canada to take for granted high or at least reasonable levels of performance by our public enterprises: the CNR, the CBC, Air Canada, Polymer, among others—perhaps Petro-Canada as well. The fact is that we know next to nothing about how they have actually performed, particularly in comparison with performance in the private sector.[17]

There is only gradually developing in Canada a tradition of journalism/scholarship in which public enterprises or public involvement in enterprise are 'muckraked' with the same diligence sometimes applied to exposés of the machinations of private corporations. Books like Philip Mathias's *Forced Growth*, Fredericks and Chambers's *Bricklin,* and Walter Stewart's *Paper Juggernaut,* offer sometimes erratic but often invaluable insights into the ways in which recent government projects have gone wrong.[18] The economists of the Fraser Institute stand poised as the most eager (and perhaps the most doctrinaire) of many policy analysts to point out to politicians the unintended harm done by such policies as rent control and wage and price controls. More substantial academic studies of government initiatives and policies of the 1960s and 1970s, such as critical appraisals of the Keynesian era of monetary and fiscal policy in Canada, are bound to follow— although it is not clear that they will keep pace with the openings given to journalists to write books about such models of enterprise as the Post Office, the British Columbia Railway, or the Liquor Control Board of Ontario.

Reappraisals of the work of the individuals involved in the expansion of government activities may also be in order, perhaps the kind of reappraisal Robert Caro carried out in his monumental study of New York's Robert Moses. [19] On the other hand, the recent biography of C.D. Howe by Robert Bothwell and William Kilbourn tends to reinforce the traditional view of Howe as a dynamic, nearly disinterested public servant achieving near-miracles through the creative use of public power. In a lengthy review of *C.D. Howe,* which elicited a vigorous reply from its authors, I have suggested that a more critical re-examination of Howe's work is called for, particularly one that questions the view that one man was responsible for the reconstruction of the Canadian economy during the war. Surely the Howe-we-won-the-war version of Canadian history needs at least the amount of critical scrutiny historians have given to the claim that bombing won the war in Europe.[20] My own study of Canadian munitions production in World War I has made me more sensitive to the problems created by the use of emergency methods of war mobilization and especially to the problem of whether or not they have any utility in peacetime.[21]

Although this survey of recent work is both selective and skimpy, it does seem to indicate that historical scholarship, perhaps following tendencies among economists, is beginning to open up the possibility of seriously questioning the role of the state in Canada as manager, regulator, and entrepreneur. We all agree that we have had a lot of state involvement; but perhaps, as Goldwin Smith suggested, we are poorer because of it. Perhaps in the future the study of Canadian history will no longer automatically reflect and reinforce the views of those who find in government activities salvation from the sins and failings of private entrepreneurs.

I do not believe. however, that such a new reading of Canadian history, even if it were to become more solidly based and widely accepted than it is now, would have any particular impact on the real world of policy formation. While personally sympathetic to the view that we have exaggerated the contribution of the state to our economic development, I am also convinced that there has seldom been and is unlikely to be any effective mobilization of private interests in favour of the contraction of the modern state. In other words, while we may come to reappraise the relative contributions of public and private enterprise in Canadian history, it will still be the case that there is no sustained, unified support in Canada for the expansion of the private sector.

To begin with a factor that profoundly colours vast areas of our consideration of the role of the state, we might remember that Canada's protective tariff was called our National Policy. It was seen and defended as an expression of Canadian nationalism. As those familiar with Goldwin Smith's work realize, his expression of free-trade beliefs in 1891 was one link in a chain of argument that equated free trade for Canada with the desirable development of a continental North American economy, and then, as another desirable consequence, with a continental nation resulting from the political union of Canada and the United States. By linking free trade with the abolition of Canada, Smith brought down upon himself the obloquy of every Canadian who was an imperialist, a nationalist, or any combination of the two. If trade liberalization really had something to do with being taken over by the United States, there was no hope of its being acceptable to Canadians. The idea of complete Canadian-American reciprocity was smeared with connotations of continentalism, annexation, even treason, and decisively rejected by the voters in the 1891 election. Even the idea of moderate reciprocity received the same treatment from nationalists in 1911 to the same effect.

The appeal to patriotism involved in maintaining the National Policy served to legitimize both the profits of those who benefited from the tariff, politicians and businessmen alike, and the losses of those who paid its price. As Aitken's phrase 'defensive expansion' reminds us, Canadian nationalism has functioned in this way as the legitimizing ideology for other Canadian policies involving positive state action, ranging from the construction of the CPR through the development of the CBC, Air Canada, the Canadian

Development Corporation, FIRA, and many other policies and institutions. Most recently the case of Petro-Canada has provided a dramatic example; nationalism, reinforcing other interests, helped to undercut utterly the Conservative and conservative case for getting the government of Canada out of the everyday business of oil production and distribution.

As well as grossly underestimating the impact Canadian nationalism would have in the Petro-Canada debate, the Conservatives also made the mistake of believing that Canadian business, especially the private oil companies, really believed in free enterprise, the limited state, and the other staples of Board of Trade after-dinner speeches. Having committed themselves to a policy on Petro-Canada that seemed designed to meet what appeared to be businessmen's deep commitment to free enterprise, the Conservatives shortly afterwards found themselves impaled on what is the real principle of business belief, which is to maximize profit. When it was in the interests of the oil industry to oppose Petro-Canada, oilmen opposed it. When it appeared to be in the industry's interests to have Petro-Canada survive, they supported it. The industry's practical consistency undercut the theoretical consistency of Conservative ideologues, tearing an enormous gap in the Clark government's credibility as well.

The advent of the National Policy in the nineteenth century was the single most significant departure from principles of free competition and free enterprise in Canadian history. Its strongest supporters were the most articulate and politically active members of the Canadian business community, gathered together in the Canadian Manufacturers Association with the avowed aim of doing all they could to foster the development of the positive state in Canada.[22] This was the most visible of many instances in which Canadian businessmen, individually and collectively, have attempted to capture the state, hoping to bring about the use of government authority to increase their incomes. Seldom in Canadian history has there been any reason for businessmen to abandon profit-maximization to chase after the laissez-faire theories, dogma, or doctrines of liberal economists. As Adam Smith realized, few businessmen ever like dangling on the strings held by the invisible hand of the free market. They looked to government to cut those strings, to liberate them from the harsh discipline of competition by taking them under its protective wing. Since the 1870s the dominant tradition in Canadian business has been to reject free-enterprise laissez-faire liberalism in favour of sheltering under the wing of an expansive, interventionist, paternalist government.[23] This essay is being written during a mild winter in Ontario. Suffering from a shortage of snow, the Ontario Ski Operators Association has petitioned the government of Ontario to spend taxpayers' money to relieve them from the consequences of a bad year. The ideology of neo-conservatism may be attracting the interest of economists and other intellectuals, but it has a long way to go in the face of businessmen who want to hold governments responsible for bad weather.

Opponents of businessmen's proclivity to snuggle around the public teat used to look to other interests for the political support necessary to implement their liberal beliefs. In the nineteenth and early twentieth centuries Canada's farmers, forced to buy on protected markets and sell on open markets, were the natural allies of free traders. But this alliance lasted only as long as farmers found free trade in their interests. After World War I gave agriculturalists an intriguing lesson in the possibilities of state marketing of their products, and after principles of enforced collective marketing spread through the agricultural community in the inter-war years, agrarian dedication to the positive, paternalist state became intense. No Canadian industry in the 1980s will be more reliant upon the state than farming.

Except, perhaps, the industries catering to our cultural needs. In the past thirty years, producers in the arts and education in Canada have replicated the earlier movements of businessmen and farmers as they have sought, been given, sought and been given still more government support for their activities. By the end of the 1970s it was virtually impossible to find an area of Canadian culture the vitality of which did not depend upon a high level of state involvement. The self-interest of cultural producers had been little different from the profit drive of widget manufacturers in impelling both groups to discard theoretical maxims about individualism and autonomy as they panted for more and more government nourishment. Nationalism proved even more effective in legitimizing self-interest when it appeared that we were being overwhelmed not just by American widgets, but by American movies, books, records, and situation comedies. By and large members of our cultural community in the 1980s will be no more willing to call for a contraction of government activities as they relate to our cultural industries—and will be no more credible if they do—than protected businessmen were when they talked about free enterprise in our manufacturing industries a century ago. Who can stand in critical judgement of state involvement in enterprises when everybody is standing in line for still more aid? As this is written, many of our Olympic athletes are pondering the consequences of having become wards of the state.

In the 1870s most Canadians did not believe governments had the competence to solve their economic problems. By the 1970s many Canadians were beginning to lose their faith in the competence of governments to solve their economic problems. Some of the trends that were discussed earlier in the essay mirror that new sentiment. It was not unlike the way in which in the 1950s we began to realize that an addiction to cigarette smoking might not be good for our health. We knew, of course, that addictions are extraordinarily hard to break no matter how well their consequences are understood in theory. They are even harder to break when they are so widely shared as to become conventional. Isolated studies, even a consensus arising from these studies—which certainly does not exist in Canada at this time—are no more likely to produce a diminution in the activities of the state than the first controversial doctors' studies were to scare people away from cigarettes. In the long run only direct realization of the real consequences of a habit is likely to scare people into trying to break it. Perhaps when Canadians come to understand the metaphorical relation between inflation and smoker's cough they will become more interested in questioning their addiction to the positive state.

NOTES

1. Goldwin Smith, *Canada and the Canadian Question* (1891; new edition, Toronto, 1971), p. 24.

2. H.G.J. Aitken, 'Defensive Expansion: The State and Economic Growth in Canada', in W.T. Easterbrook and M.H. Watkins, eds, *Approaches to Canadian Economic History* (Toronto, 1967), p. 184.

3. Herschel Hardin, *A Nation Unaware: The Canadian Economic Culture* (Vancouver, 1974).

4. While that supposition does no harm to this essay, it may not be correct. Assumptions about the differing roles of the state in Canada and the United States usually fail to adjust for different stages in chronological development and differences in the ways in which state power is used in vastly differing economies.

5. The best historiographical treatment of the National Policy is still chapter 7 of J.H. Dales, *The Protective Tariff in Canada's Development* (Toronto, 1966). Dales does not, however, trace the National Policy myth-making back to its roots, the chief of which appears to be O.D. Skelton's treatment of it in his *General Economic History of the Dominion, 1867-1912 (Canada and its Provinces* series, Toronto, 1913). The last classic polemic against the National Policy was J.R. Porritt's *Sixty Years of Protection in Canada* (Winnipeg, 1908; revised edition 1913).

6. Dales, *The Protective Tariff.*

7. Nationalists have viewed with alarm the evidence of branch-plant-inducing effects cited by Michael Bliss, 'Canadianizing American Business: The Roots of the Branch Plant', in Ian Lumsden, ed., *Close the 49th Parallel* (Toronto, 1970). Other scholars have pointed out, however, that many of these plants would have located in Canada anyway and that there were other Canadian policies at least as attractive to foreign investors. The anti-tariff views implicit in Tom Naylor's *History of Canadian Business, 1867-1914* (2 vols, Toronto, 1975) are discussed in my critical review of that work in *Historie Sociale/Social History*, 18 (November 1976), and not disavowed by Naylor in his reply in the following issue.

8. *Journal of Canadian Studies*, 14, 3 (Fall 1979).

9. H.V. Nelles, 'The Ties That Bind: Berton's CPR', *Canadian Forum*, November-December 1970.

10. P.J. George, 'Rates of Return in Railway investment and Implications for Government Subsidization of the CPR: Some Preliminary Results', *Canadian Journal of Economics*, 1, 4 (November 1968). For the ensuing controversy see vol. 6, 3 (August 1973), and vol. 8, 4 (November 1975).

11. Kenneth H. Norrie, 'The National Policy and the Rate of Prairie Settlement: A Review', *Journal of Canadian Studies*, 14, 3 (Fall 1979), p. 72.

12. Ralph Allen, *Ordeal by Fire: 1915-1945* (Toronto, 1961).

13. G.R. Stevens, *Canadian National Railways* (Toronto, 1962), vol. 2, chapters 1-9.

14. T.D. Regehr, *The Canadian Northern Railway* (Toronto, 1976); Albro Martin, *Enterprise Denied: Origins of the Decline of American Railroads, 1897-1917* (New York, 1971).

15. H.V. Nelles, *The Politics of Development: Forests, Mines & Hydro-Electric Power in*

Ontario, 1849-1941 (Toronto, 1974), p. ix; for the Marxist view see the essays by Leo Panitch and Reg Whitaker in Panitch, ed., *The Canadian State: Political Economy and Political Power* (Toronto, 1977).

16. Nelles, *The Politics of Development*, p. 413; see also Nelles, 'Public Ownership of Electrical Utilities in Manitoba and Ontario', *Canadian Historical Review*, LVII, 4 (December 1976).

17. The only book-length study of Crown corporations in Canada is C.A. Ashley and R.G.H. Smails, *Canadian Crown Corporations: Some Aspects of Their Administration and Control* (Toronto, 1965); the beginnings of an informed appraisal of Polymer and several other enterprises are contained in Michael R. Graham, *Canada Development Corporation* (Study No. 4 of the Royal Commission on Corporate Concentration, Ottawa 1977). Much of the enthusiasm for the CNR's early years derives from the hagiographic biography by D'Arcy Marsh, *The Tragedy of Henry Thornton* (Toronto, 1935); a very different view is summarized in Michael Bliss, *A Canadian Millionaire: The Life and Business Times of Sir Joseph Flavelle, Bart, 1858-1939* (Toronto, 1978), pp. 482-3.

18. Philip Mathias, *Forced Growth: Five Studies of Government Involvement in the Development of Canada* (Toronto, 1971); H.A. Fredericks and Allan Chambers, *Bricklin* (Fredericton, 1977); Walter Stewart, *Paper Juggernaut: Big Government Gone Mad* (Toronto, 1979).

19. Robert Caro, *The Power Broker: Robert Moses and the Fall of New York* (New York, 1974); the suggestion of Canadian comparisons is made in my review in *Canadian Forum* (April-May 1975).

20. Robert Bothwell and William Kilbourn, *C.D. Howe* (Toronto, 1979); Michael Bliss, 'The Legacy of C.D. Howe', *Canadian Business* (Nov. 1979); authors' reply, *Canadian Business* (Jan. 1980).

21. Bliss, *A Canadian Millionaire*, chapters 10-16.

22. For manufacturers' views on the tariff see Michael Bliss, *A Living Profit* (Toronto, 1974), ch. 5; the authoritative study of the advent of the National Policy is now Ben Forster, 'The Coming of the National Policy: Business, Government and the Tariff, 1876-1879,' *Journal of Canadian Studies*, 14, 3 (Autumn 1979).

23. The rejection of liberalism by business and other groups in Canadian society is a leit-motiv of *A Living Profit* and *A Canadian Millionaire*, and is addressed directly, if somewhat confusedly, in Bliss, 'The Protective Impulse: an Approach to the Social History of Oliver Mowat's Ontario', in Don Swainson, ed., *Oliver Mowat's Ontario* (Toronto, 1972). The classic formulation is Karl Polanyi's *The Great Transformation: The Political and Economic Origins of Our Time* (Boston, 1944).

H.V. Nelles

CANADIAN ENERGY POLICY, 1945-1980: A FEDERALIST PERSPECTIVE

There are some things we can't have and probably don't need. One of them is a national energy policy. Our constitution practically forbids it and our unique resource endowments render it superfluous, perhaps even counter-productive. In this essay I will argue that *for a consideration* the federal government ought to retreat from the field it has occupied during the last two decades, leaving energy policy in the hands of the provinces where it formerly lay and where it more properly belongs.

My point of departure for this line of argument is Professor Alan Cairns's provocative essay, 'The Other Crisis of Canadian Federalism'.[1] In that paper Cairns directs our attention beyond the immediate question of Quebec's place in Canada to an equally fundamental challenge to federalism, the paralysis that results from the perpetual conflict of dirigist federal and provincial governments. 'We have reached the stage', Cairns writes, 'where the necessity of intergovernmental co-ordination and collaboration is not matched with an equivalent capacity for its attainment.' The collision of big battalions of officials with different objectives has become the normal rather than the exceptional case as governments at both levels have bureaucratized and begun planning in earnest. 'We are left with an overloaded political system which has gotten out of control, a system of competitive big governments which, increasingly incapable of effective governing, burdens the societies it is supposed to serve.' Untangling this web of government, Cairns argues, is the most urgent problem facing students of Canadian politics.

Perhaps part of the burden of government to which Cairns makes reference could be lifted if we tried to identify some areas of separate federal and provincial responsibility that would not require major constitutional reform. Such an effort might not succeed in carving out completely distinct compartments of juris-diction, but it might serve to reverse somewhat the recent tendency for both levels of government to get hopelessly wound up in each other's affairs with a consequent loss of time, temper, decisiveness, and belief in the efficacy of politics. In this instance I suggest returning primacy in the energy field to the provinces. They have the resources, the bureaucrats, and the planning capability. The most obvious costs would involve a loss of interprovincial unifor-mity in prices (a relatively recent idea that has never been realized), a profusion of regional plans with a corresponding loss of admi-nistrative neatness and overriding central control, and of necessity some violation of equity on the energy account. That might not be too high a price to pay and might be compensated for in another way.

I

Since the end of the war the federal government has conducted at least six major surveys of the Canadian energy situation. Review-ing these largely forgotten documents for this essay, I was reminded how quickly and dramatically circumstances have changed in the last thirty-five years and how rarely investigators have anticipated these developments. Looking backward from the 1980s, at a time when electricity, coal, and even wood are staging comebacks, we can also see how relatively brief the oil age was. Nor should we imagine that change has stopped or that we can see the future any more clearly now. Economists may have grown less cautious about their projections; that does not mean we should place any more confidence in them.

C.D. Howe launched the first of these energy studies in 1944 when he appointed a Royal Commission to make recommend-ations regarding the postwar stabilization of the historically troubled Canadian coal industry. Naturally the commissioners had to peer ahead, calculating future energy needs and estimating the position of coal vis-à-vis its substitutes in the coming dispensa-tion. Although the commissioners commented upon the close correlation of employment levels and energy demand, they shrank from making any systematic projections. They contented themselves with the bland observation: 'Energy requirements have declined slowly from the peak of 1944 and will probably continue to decline for a time. What will follow then we do not know.'[2]

Since coal accounted for fifty-seven per cent of Canada's primary energy requirements in 1945, the Royal Commission guessed that it would continue to hold its own against its competitors. Oil would make some inroads in transportation and space heating, but its price guaranteed that it would continue to be 'a luxury fuel'. Depletion of the Turner Valley field in Alberta hinted at possible oil-supply difficulties on the Prairies, but other parts of Canada could easily be served by abundant foreign products. Neither of the major railroads reported any plans to convert from steam to diesel engines. Thus, after taking the likely price and availability of oil into account and discounting its penetration of the space-heating market, the commissioners arrived fairly confidently at the conclusion: 'Despite the importance of alternative sources of energy, coal is, and will probably continue to be the most important source of energy for railway locomotives and for industrial and domestic heating.'[3]

They couldn't have been more wrong. After 1948 coal fell into a steep decline. Oil displaced it *most* rapidly in transportation and in residential and commercial applications. The railroads changed their minds with uncharacteristic speed, for in less than a decade steam engines all but disappeared from mainline service. Furnaces were converted wholesale to the cleaner, more easily handled fuel; cars, trucks, and buses resumed their triumphant progress. Falling world oil prices, rising personal incomes, and of course Leduc completely overturned the Coal Commission's hesitant predictions. As it turned out, coal consumption actually dropped by seventeen per cent over the next decade as oil consumption tripled. Studies carried out in the mid-fifties concluded that since the war coal had fallen from supplying fifty-seven per cent of Canadian primary energy requirements to thirty-one per cent, while oil had risen from twenty-one to forty-nine per cent, replacing it as far and away the most important energy source.[4] An entirely unexpected energy revolution had occurred.

This sudden substitution of oil for coal also produced a new form of energy analysis. Up to this point economists had focused their attention on individual energy sources, such as coal. The fifties required a new strategy, analysis of the entire interlocking pattern of energy supplies. The simultaneous emergence of developmental economics, a scholarly fascination with the process of economic growth, and a mounting American concern about the security of essential industrial raw materials facilitated this shift from the study of resources in isolation, such as coal, to the changing components of energy supply and demand.[5] In Canada John Davis conducted one of the first of these comprehensive energy studies for the Gordon Commission on Canada's Economic Prospects. The Davis report, *Canadian Energy Prospects*, published in the spring of 1957, can still be read with profit as one of the boldest, most informative, and most carefully reasoned studies made of the subject. It assembled for the first time reliable historical statistics of energy consumption, examined each supply sector in detail, explored the linkage of rising GNP and rising energy consumption at home and abroad, and on the basis of these and other data hazarded a sophisticated prediction of Canadian energy supply and use to the year 1980.

Writing amidst the buoyant optimism of the mid-fifties, reflecting the prevailing mood that at last everything was possible, Davis reported that Canada possessed more than enough energy, especially oil, to meet its soaring needs. He concluded that Canada had conventional oil reserves 'adequate to cover Canadian requirements for several centuries', and that if the Tar Sands were included in the calculations Canada's needs could be met 'for something like a thousand years'.[6] Electricity alone was a source of worry, for by the seventies most hydro-electric power would be economical enough to step in, especially in Eastern Canada. Over all, Canada was moving extremely rapidly from a condition of dependence on foreign energy to self-sufficiency, and appeared headed for a major role as an energy exporter for the first time. By 1980, for example, Davis estimated that Canada would be producing approximately three million barrels of oil a day and shipping more than half of it to the United States. (In fact actual production in 1980 is running closer to 1.2 million barrels a day.) The biggest problem seemed to be locating markets big enough to justify large-scale development of Canada's superabundant energy reserves. That meant exports of oil, gas, and even electricity. 'Energy in a physical sense, is not likely to be a scarce commodity,' Davis concluded comfortingly. 'Neither will it become unduly expensive.' Energy demand was expected to grow at a rate of 4.25 per cent annually, making the energy sector itself a significant motor of broader Canadian economic growth.[7]

Davis's finding meshed nicely with the boundless confidence that resonated through both the *Preliminary* and the *Final Report* of the Gordon Commission on Canada's Economic Prospects. In the former, release of which on the eve of a general election caused such a furor, the commissioners expressed great satisfaction at the steeply rising demand expected for energy, in particular for oil and gas, which were projected to account for between two-thirds and three-quarters of the total energy required in 1980. 'In both of these commodities,' the *Preliminary Report* stated, 'Canada will on balance be more than self-sufficient.' The future seemed dazzling in contrast to a record of poor economic performance and a history of energy dependence. Resource abundance and capital scarcity thus led the Gordon Commission to recommend a policy of extensive energy exports: 'we should seek more or less immediate markets at reasonable prices for our oil and other materials,' Gordon and his colleagues argued, 'in order that the present generation may receive some of the benefits from them and in order to ensure the continuation of the present rapid pace of development in our oil industry.'[8]

The *Final Report* of the Gordon Commission, written mainly by Douglas LePan, proclaimed energy the 'orb and sceptre' of man's 'sovereignty over nature'. That being the case, Canada seemed destined for ever greater dominion. In the new era of economic prosperity that lay ahead the Commission forecast 'a great increase in the production, consumption and export of oil and natural gas'. But for once the *Final Report* was more cautious, more openly hedonistic, than the Davis study upon which it drew (evidence perhaps of LePan's sardonic influence): 'Our resources of these fossil fuels, although very large, are not of course inexhaustible; and it may be that in retrospect the period will seem little more than an interlude. But it promises to be a great feast while it lasts.'[9]

Energy abundance and the necessity of securing large export markets to sustain development were also the guiding themes of the next major energy review which followed hot on the heels of the Gordon Commission. The Royal Commission on Energy, appointed by the incoming Diefenbaker government to sort out the contentious issue of pipeline construction and finance, conducted a detailed survey of Canadian oil and gas reserves, production, transmission, current and potential markets. In two reports highly critical of the sharp financial practices of the pipeline's promoters, the Borden Commission on Energy arrived at three basic conclusions: (1) that a National Energy Board should be set up to advise the federal government on energy questions and to regulate exports; (2) that ample supplies of oil and gas existed surplus to Canada's needs, that existing export applications should be approved, and that further markets in the United States should be vigorously sought; and (3) that the domestic market west of the Ottawa River should be reserved for western Canadian crude.[10] Although sympathetic to the nationalist arguments advanced by Home Oil and the independent Canadian producers—whose markets were limited by American import quotas—that the Montreal market should also be opened up to western oil, Borden and his colleagues somewhat reluctantly disagreed. Analysis of comparative transmission cost, either via a publicly or privately built pipeline or through an expanded Interprovincial system, all pointed to the same basic conclusion: Alberta crude could not compete with foreign oil in Montreal without subsidies, tariffs, import restrictions and a willingness on the part of Quebec consumers to pay higher prices. The multinational refiners in Montreal also protested, preferring to run down their own high-profit offshore oil reserves rather than develop more expensive Canadian holdings or purchase Canadian crude at arm's length from their competitors.[11]

The Diefenbaker government eventually accepted most of the Borden Commission's recommendations. In 1959 a National Energy Board was established to regulate the construction and operation of interprovincial pipelines and international powerlines, to monitor energy production and advise the cabinet on energy-related issues, and to license trade in gas, oil, and electricity subject to cabinet approval. On the controversial question of protecting Canadian oil produceers against foreign competititon the government procrastinated. Then in 1961 George Hees, the minister of trade and commerce, proclaimed a National Oil Policy whose primary goal was to promote the expansion of the western Canadian oil industry by reserving to it an exclusive portion of the eastern Canadian market. A line was drawn down the Ottawa Valley. West of this line imports would be displaced by domestic supplies. East of the line Quebec and the Atlantic region would continue to be served by imported, mainly Venezuelan, crude. Thus the Canadian petroleum market was divided roughly in half between foreign and domestic suppliers. The National Oil Policy, which operated on a voluntary basis for almost a decade, also effectively established a two-price system. Consumers east of the Ottawa Valley line paid less for imports than the domestic prices prevailing west of the line. Oil exports were also officially encouraged, but the controlling factor was American reluctance to buy rather than Canadian eagerness to sell. Thus the pace of oil exploration and development in Canada would be governed by the growth of demand for petroleum in Ontario and the American oil import quota levels.[12]

Despite this double confinement the western Canadian oil and gas industries flourished primarily because of surging energy consumption in the 1960s. As predicted, energy in all forms was abundant and cheap. Total energy consumption grew at an average annual rate of 5.6 per cent compared with 5.4 per cent for the economy as a whole. Natural gas and petroleum led the parade. [13] Affluence, an economic boom, and rising exports sucked up enormous quantities of gas, oil, and hydro-electricity. The great energy barbecue was on. Canada, on account of its energy intensive industrial structure, climate, dispersed housing patterns, and automotive-based transportation system, rose to second place among the world's leading per-capita energy users. In 1972 Canada overtook the United States, a dubious lead it has maintained ever since.[14]

Curiously, this galloping appetite for energy caused little concern at the time. The idealistic, self-indulgent sixties were not years for that sort of introspection. Material abundance was assumed. Medicare, social security, discrimination, Quebec, personal liberation, foreign investment, poverty, war—those were the burning questions. Energy was judged to be sufficiently well studied and supplied not to require a Royal Commission or even a

Task Force during the decade. Meantime, the lights were left on, parking lots expanded, and we built for a future in which it was expected that energy would be a negligible expense. Even as late as 1970 blithe assurances about virtually limitless supplies guided the National Energy Board in its decisions on export applications.[15] In 1971 Joe Greene, acting as Canada's energy salesman, sought to impress some potential American customers in Denver with Canada's 390 years of oil and 932 years of natural gas in place.[16] It was, as the Gordon Commission had promised, a glorious feast.

It had to end, of course, and we all remember that it did even if we can't recall the details. Even before OPEC and the oil embargo doubts began to accumulate. The life of Canada's proven gas reserves began to fall in 1966, a decline that accelerated with steeply rising demand. In 1970, for the first time, oil exploration failed to replenish reserves as quickly as they were being drawn down.[17] The Alberta government began to realize that its known conventional petroleum resources might not last beyond the mid-eighties. Oil prices, which had been falling in real terms since the fifties, began to creep upward as domestic and international supplies gradually tightened. Representatives of the major oil-exporting countries met in Caracas in 1970 and Tehran in 1971 to plot a common strategy to take advantage of the seller's market which was developing primarily as a result of the growing U.S. dependence on foreign supplies.[18] In Eastern Canada the provincial electric utilities made plans for massive new thermal, nuclear, and hydro-electric stations to keep pace with a demand they estimated to be growing at close to seven per cent annually.[19]

During this delicate transitional period in world energy markets, the federal government launched another comprehensive review of Canadian needs and resources. The result, *An Energy Policy For Canada: Phase 1*, released in the early summer of 1973, can be read as one of the last documents of the sixties. Its assumptions and concerns were those of the great barbecue rather than the decade of uncertainty. The anonymous authors explicitly took it for granted that high per-capita energy consumption was essential to the good life in Canada. Accordingly, it was the task of government, especially the federal government, to ensure that these energy needs were adequately supplied. The policy challenges that lay ahead would not arise from a shortage of either energy resources or technology, but rather from the economic impact of satisfying needs on such a scale. Meeting projected coal, oil, gas, and electrical demand would have major implications for the environment, would require staggering amounts of capital, could increase already unacceptable levels of foreign ownership in the energy sector, and threatened to integrate Canada more thoroughly into a continental energy market. To accommodate demand *An Energy Policy For Canada* proposed five packages—of pipelines, tar-sands plants, frontier and offshore oil and gas developments—which would provide varying degrees of self-sufficiency in the two key forms of energy which were expected to continue to account for eighty per cent of all consumption up to 1990. The cost, depending upon the option taken and its timing, ranged upwards to a daunting $85 billion, or almost six per cent of estimated GNP throughout the remainder of the seventies.

To mitigate some of the distressing side-effects of development on such a scale, the EMR report recommended stiffer terms and conditions for federal oil and gas leases, beefed-up nuclear and synthetic oil research efforts, upgraded exports embodying energy rather than exporting raw energy, and finally the formation of a national oil company to conduct international transactions and to expand the bridgehead of Canadian ownership in this all-important sector of the economy. The challenge was enormous, but the job could be done, EMR concluded confidently: 'Canada has more than enough energy resources available to cover her own use at least until the year 2050 and . . . there is a chance that there may be substantial amounts of oil and gas surplus to domestic demand.'[20]

Events in the fall of 1973 rendered this report obsolete more rapidly than most. OPEC's success at winning a series of huge oil-price increases effectively wrecked the old National Oil Policy, and demanded an immediate response. The federal government, then in a minority position, acted to insulate Canada from this oil shock first by restricting and taxing exports to subsidize imports, secondly by undertaking to guarantee the availability of oil and gas across Canada at a single price—a step unprecedented in peacetime—and thirdly by establishing that price through negotiation with the oil-producing provinces. On the supply side pipelines were planned to move Arctic gas south, and at long last the Interprovincial oil pipeline was extended to Montreal. A national oil company, Petro-Canada, was launched; Syncrude was refinanced at gunpoint with public money; and exploration on the frontier was accelerated. Energy conservation programs were set in motion to dampen rising demand, which was now thought to be incompatible with the good life—or at least the warm life in winter. The federal government also passed the Petroleum Administration Act in 1975 to provide for the rationing of scarce supplies in the event of an emergency and to permit unilateral action in anticipation of failure to reach an agreement on price with the producing provinces. The net effect of this vigorous federal intervention was to hold Canadian energy prices well below world levels, but thereby to internalize in the form of sharp federal-provincial conflict the struggle raging internationally between oil importing and exporting countries.[21]

Naturally the energy-producing provinces sought to make the most of their new-found advantage. Alberta and Saskatchewan quickly raised their oil and gas royalties and revised their leasing policies to capture the lion's share of these windfall gains. They also established Crown corporations to participate directly in new resource development, and Alberta put a provincial oil and gas marketing commission in place to strengthen its resource ownership claim and thus its control over price. Both provinces resented federal intrusion into what they considered to be their jurisdiction over natural resources and bitterly resisted federal efforts in 1974 to lay claim to a bigger portion of these greatly enhanced energy revenues. They fought relentlessly in a series of interminable conferences for domestic prices closer to world levels in order to promote conservation of diminishing stocks and rejuvenate exploration for new reserves. In this campaign Alberta and Saskatchewan were supported by virtually all the economists in the country, led by the Economic Council and the C.D. Howe Research Institute, which deplored such political distortion of the market and the contribution of the Oil Import Compensation Programme to the mounting federal deficit.[22]

The federal government justified its actions, revised its forecasts, and laid down new, more hesitant goals in the second energy review of the decade, published in 1976. Compared to those that had come before, *An Energy Strategy For Canada* was a report filled with doubt. Now the energy picture looked much bleaker than it had only three years earlier. Gone were the assumptions of abundance. Gone too was the conviction that energy would be, or for that matter ought to be, cheap. Writing on energy, therefore, faithfully reflected the much deeper crisis of confidence that marked the seventies. Now EMR cautiously admitted that there *might* be enough energy to meet projected needs, or thought that it might be found, but that it would most certainly prove more difficult and more costly to locate and move to market than anyone had previously believed. Merely to maintain existing production, prices would have to increase. If current consumption patterns persisted, this report concluded grimly, supplies of oil and gas would not be adequate to meet demand. At low prices there might be enough coal and electricity to get by, but gas and oil reserves would run down alarmingly fast. Even at much higher prices and with extraordinary investment in exploration and development, expensive, insecure imports would be needed throughout the eighties to supplement Canadian production until new reserves could be brought on stream. *An Energy Strategy For Canada* forecast imminent shortfalls of natural gas and petroleum in both its high and its low price projections. Even as this report was being prepared, Canadian oil production—which had been declining since 1973 and has continued to drop ever since—fell below domestic needs. In 1976 Canada became a net importer of oil, as it had been before 1968.

According to this report, Canadians faced a discouraging future of grave and expensive choices. Energy was running out. It would take billions of dollars to find and develop new supplies. In the meantime, energy consumption would have to be brought under strict control. Even a minimum program of energy self-reliance would require much higher energy prices, drastic conservation measures, redoubled exploration and development, conversion from scarce to more readily available fuels, the construction of a host of pipelines, nuclear reactors, thermal generating stations, and power lines, and a much more determined research effort on the intractable tar sands. Moreover, these capital projects would also have to be reconciled with other concerns that had asserted themselves in the seventies: native rights, the environmental impact of energy corridors, nuclear safety, security from terrorism, and acid rain—all of which would require more time and cost more money. In short, there was no easy fix.

Thus, *An Energy Strategy For Canada* marked the end of an era of cheap and abundant energy. It also became the basis for a revised federal energy policy. With varying degrees of conviction the Trudeau and Clark governments set out to raise Canadian prices closer to world levels, decried oil imports, and aimed for energy self-sufficiency by 1990. A generation accustomed to thinking there was enough energy to last for centuries grudgingly adjusted. By degrees the sweaters went on, the lights went out, cars got smaller, attics were insulated, and once again the furnace became the object of resentment it had formerly been.[23]

To drive these grim lessons home Energy, Mines, and Resources issued its third energy forecast of the decade, *Energy Futures For Canadians,* in 1978. With much heavy underlining and many bold charts, the LEAP (Long-Term Energy Assessment Programme) report underscored the deterioration of the Canadian energy situation. In a text liberally sprinkled with words like 'crisis', 'uncertainty', 'precarious', and 'critical', the authors warned that 'the long term future is urgent.' The crunch and its wrenching adjustments would come in 1985 and after. Even under a crash program involving the construction of ten tar-sands plants in the West and twice as many nuclear reactors in the East, energy self-reliance would have to be pushed back to the year 2000. 'Reduce' and 'replace' were the twin themes of this report: reduce energy consumption below a 5.5 per cent annual growth rate, and replace oil with more plentiful indigenous substitutes. To achieve self-reliance by the turn of the century the LEAP report set a series of performance targets and proposed a package of programs, the most important of which called for quadrupling coal production; increasing domestic oil production by fifty per cent, mainly by shifting to heavy oil and synthetic petroleum; and raising the nuclear share of the most rapidly expanding electrical supply sector from four per cent in 1975 to thirty per cent by 2000. Meeting basic energy needs in the years ahead would be 'the most demanding task undertaken by Canadians in peacetime'.[24]

It comes as something of a surprise, after reading these alarming documents, to enter the 1980s with a surplus of energy. Canada *is* energy self-sufficient. Throughout the seventies Canada ran a balance-of-payments surplus on its energy account of well over a billion dollars annually. We bought oil and sold natural gas, coal, and electricity, and had billions to spare. Indeed, there is a very real danger of over-expanding surpluses on this account to remedy other balance-of-payments difficulties, thereby becoming a continental energy supplier—a role, incidentally, which would distort the economy and rapidly deplete our resources.[25]

Ironically, our present problem is a surplus of energy. Canada has quite a lot more coal than it needs.[26] So much natural gas has recently been found that the independent gas producers of Alberta desperately need to clear the market of the excess. The National Energy Board has approved export applications—the first since 1970—but for the moment the United States is balking at the price.[27] Eastern Canada has too much electricity. Consumption has levelled off so sharply in Ontario on account of slower economic growth and mass conservation that some generating stations are being mothballed and others shut down for extensive repairs, and the whole nuclear program has been put on the back burner for the time being. Ontario Hydro has been both damned for this expensive miscalculation and praised for having such a prodigious surplus on hand that it can be sold to the U.S. at a profit. Quebec, as is well known, is counting on customers for its James Bay power in New York. Meanwhile, the premier of Manitoba has put off further northern hydro-electric development for want of markets.[28] Finally, we are not importing an appreciably greater volume of oil in the late seventies than we did earlier in the decade.[29] These imports might be cause for some concern, but they hardly warrant the military metaphors of the last two Energy, Mines, and Resources reports. Much more to the point, in coal, gas, and electricity we are stumbling towards a continental energy market with our surpluses. As a study prepared for the U.S. Senate Committee on Energy and Natural Resources recently revealed: 'The hemispheric energy system already exists.'[30] It is all very confusing, but it should not be surprising.

II

Energy forecasting, even for the short term, has proven an extremely tricky and misleading business. That has been the main point of this lengthy meander through thirty-five years of energy investigations in Canada. The demonstrated unreliability of energy projections throws a long shadow over any proposal for centralized planning based upon them. What would have been the outcome of an energy strategy that relied upon the Coal Commission's assessment of the postwar competitiveness of oil? What has been the consequence of depending upon the oft-repeated assertions of the infinite availability of petroleum? Should we place any greater confidence, therefore, in the more melancholy recent studies which have greatly underestimated current supplies and the impact of higher prices and conservation on consumption?

Energy forecasts are only as good as the assumptions that lie behind them. How seriously should we take the urgent recommendations of *Energy Futures For Canadians,* for example, which make no allowance for additions to conventional oil reserves either in Alberta or offshore?[31] During the eighteen months since the publication of this report there have been four major discoveries of strategically placed commercial oil pools: West Pembina, Bow Island, Ben Nevis, and Hibernia.[32] To take another example, could the eastern electrical utilities justify pressing ahead with an expensive nuclear-power program, something that Energy, Mines, and Resources thought essential on the basis of 1975 figures, in the face of such enormous electricity surpluses? Some of the pessimism that pervades recent energy assessments seems to come from discounting the possibility of short-run change and placing too much weight on long-term projections. It might be said that this is taking the short-term view. I would agree, short-term but not necessarily shortsighted. There is nothing in the history of energy forecasting to warrant placing great confidence in long-term projections.

The inability to predict domestic conditions, much less world trends, raises serious doubt about the efficacy of centralized planning. The energy situation is still too capricious, contingencies too likely—especially with oil. Prices have risen more rapidly than anyone would have thought possible. The international supply picture has changed dramatically with political revolutions and shifting consumption patterns. Currently, for example, there is an international oil glut.[33] In such circumstances short-term prediction is chancy, long-term planning essentially an academic exercise.

Nor does the U.S. experience with a national energy policy up to the mid-seventies offer much reassurance. The American import quota system, administered gas pricing at the wellhead, and emergency allocation efforts during the embargo have been subjected to extensive scholarly and political criticism. The most authoritative study of U.S. energy-supply management arrives at the surprising conclusion that the Federal Energy Office may well have created shortages of oil and inspired needless panic in the spring of 1974. Planners simply could not cope with the regional complexities of a market as large as that of the United States. With regard to U.S. energy policy before 1974, Richard B. Mancke concluded:

> As the costly failures of such policies as natural gas wellhead price ceilings, mandatory oil import controls illustrate, whenever there is considerable uncertainty about future conditions affecting a regulated industry, it is poor strategy to blindly adhere to an inflexible policy whose success depends upon the occurrence of a specific and frequently unlikely chain of events. Instead, a flexible groping strategy is advisable.[34]

Effective national planning presupposes a high degree of certainty. It works best in a relatively stable environment. Neither predictability nor stability characterizes the Canadian energy situation.

Nevertheless, the perils of short-term forecasting and the failure of U.S. energy policies notwithstanding, all the Canadian energy reviews of the seventies called for greater centralized planning in one form or another. The first, second, and third Energy, Mines, and Resources studies called for 'a national energy policy', 'a national energy strategy', and 'a national energy programme' respectively. The Science Council has advocated the creation of a National Resources Management Authority. As we have seen, the federal government has taken charge of oil and gas pricing and supply management, drawn more by immediate political considerations than by any well-thought-out plan. No longer can it be said, as the 1973 energy review stated, that centralized control of energy is not in the Canadian tradition.[35] Most commentators want to expand the federal role. Professor Moore of UBC made such a case in the 1975 British Columbia Institute for Economic Policy Analysis conference on Natural Resource Revenues. Most recently Professor Ian McDougall, of Osgoode Hall Law School, in a paper presented at Harvard University, argued on behalf of a Federal Energy Marketing Board.[36] In characteristically extravagant fashion, *Energy Futures For Canadians* justifies an enhanced federal role on the higher ground of national unity: 'A national energy programme can become a functional, national link for mutual benefit, much like the railroad did one hundred years ago.'[37]

The problem, of course, is that a national energy policy by whatever name could also be as divisive as the railroad. Upon close examination, most of the elements of these national energy policies turn out to lie within provincial jurisdiction. The provinces own their oil, gas, tar sands, coal, and waterpower. They also have to pay for the nuclear and thermal generating stations that have been so grandly proposed. The provinces also control automobile licensing, gasoline taxation, highway tolls, electrical-rate schedules, building codes, sales taxes, and property taxes. In short, the provinces regulate the most effective policy levers on energy production and consumption. Further federal intrusion would necessarily conflict with prior provincial competence. The Energy, Mines, and Resources studies usually noted this in passing, implying that these differences would melt away through co-operation, co-ordination, or some other euphemism for prolonged intergovernmental hostility. I am not convinced. As my colleague Professor Smiley pointed out at the 1975 Victoria conference, in a federal system characterized by autonomous though highly interdependent governments, achieving 'a high degree of rationality in Canadian resource policy is impossible'.[38] That being the case, I am inclined to suggest the contrary; namely, that the provinces be reminded of their responsibility and permitted to exercise their ample jurisdiction with a minimum of outside direction or interference.

Technically the federal government does have the constitutional authority to supplant the provinces in the energy field. The declaratory power could be used to declare the oil and gas wells, pipelines, power plants, and transmission lines for the general advantage of Canada and thereby move them under federal jurisdiction. This has happened to western utilities before. If grain elevators and BC Tel are for the general advantage of Canada, surely the oil and gas wells are too? But simply to advance such an argument is to refute it. This would amount to a federal coup d'état. It would have to be carried out over the strenuous objection of not only the producing provinces, but also the principal consuming provinces, Ontario and Quebec, who have their own historical reasons for resisting federal jurisdictional aggrandizement.[39] Alternatively, the trade and commerce power could be interpreted in the federal government's favour, as it was in the opaque decision handed down by the Supreme Court in the CIGOL vs. the Government of Saskatchewan case.[40] Or the emergency power could be stretched to justify a national energy program just as it was for wage and price controls.

All of this is possible under our existing constitutional arrangements, but I think undesirable. There is no real or apprehended emergency. Is the long-term future so urgent or so certain as to warrant a constitutional revolution? I think not. Perhaps the goals of the various national energy policies could be achieved more peacefully, if a little less gracefully, by other means. Energy can be regulated at the provincial level. All the provinces have experienced their quiet revolutions, as Professor Cairns has demonstrated. They are now thoroughly bureaucratized, fully capable of generating and administering complex social and economic plans, and, if interfered with, equally well fitted out for protracted combat. Each one has an energy commission of some sort. Most provinces have published elaborate surveys of energy production and consumption to rival their federal counterparts.[41] Should not provinces be left to do the job?

A comparison of energy use in industrial countries recently published by the Canadian Energy Research Institute of Calgary shows that Canada is relatively energy-efficient—taking into account its industrial structure—in all but the transportation sector. Here, of course, the culprit is the automobile. Canadians drive their cars about the same distance annually as motorists in other countries, but we own more cars per capita and they are larger here than anywhere else.[42] The automobile will have to be taken in hand. In such a matter touching upon questions of taste and personal freedom, perhaps the province is the level where the costs and benefits should be weighed. Certainly the province, with its control over roads, tolls, licences, registration, and direct taxation, is best equipped to legislate effectively. Moreoever, providing energy in the future will require making choices between competing forms of energy. Will coal or nuclear energy drive the electric turbines once waterpower has been fully developed? Such contentious questions are best left to the local government. Provinces with different resource endowments and political traditions might well follow different paths, and, as a result, pay different prices.[43] The provincial legislatures should take responsibility for lowering speed limits, taxing gas guzzlers, and making the difficult choice between the acid rain of coal-fired electrical generation or glowing in the dark with nuclear power.

I am also persuaded that the energy-producing provinces ought to be able to set the price for their dwindling resources and capture as much of their rent as they consider proper. No fair-minded person can take issue with Premier Lougheed's determination to obtain the best terms possible for a rapidly depleting resource. After all, Leduc No. 1 ran dry two years ago and is now a non-revenue-producing historic site. The government of Alberta's expressed aim of using oil and gas revenue to assist in the diversification of the western economy also commands wide support. We can all share the concern of the governments of Alberta and Saskatchewan not to allow energy-related projects to rip apart the social fabric or overheat the economy unduly. Yet thus far federal energy policies have implicitly frustrated some of those objectives, and with predictable results. There is no justification for assuming greater federal expertise in either energy development or pricing policies. In the Syncrude case Professors Helliwell and May have demonstrated the contrary.[44] The producing provinces are probably better judges of appropriate development strategies, and certainly better negotiators than the federal government. In this Alberta could cite a long list of disputes between Ontario and the federal government over conflicting development ambitions.[45]

According to Professor Scott's analysis, it makes little difference from the point of view of economic efficiency whether the federal or the provincial government collects the resource rent.[46] At present the province has the clearer jurisdiction. It has been argued that it makes sense for the resource manager to act as rent collector as well. Let us then leave it to British Columbia, Alberta, and

Saskatchewan to set the prices at which they wish their resources to be sold, and capture an appropriate portion of the rents taking into account the imperatives of further exploration, research, and development. The federal-provincial conference is not an ideal setting for determining energy prices. This forum should concern itself with other, more explicitly intergovernmental matters which I will turn to in a moment.

Oil and gas are the first of the great staple products that have dominated Canadian development which have been consumed primarily in the home market. Heretofore we have followed the world price of fish, fur, forest products, and wheat primarily as producers rather than consumers. Were the federal government to withdraw from oil and gas price-fixing, the cost to the Canadian consumer of the former at least would undoubtedly rise. But how fast and how high remains an open question. The energy-producing provinces do not exist in a vacuum. They are highly integrated in a national economy whose well-being is also their intimate concern. There is no reason to believe that once freed of direct federal control these provinces will behave as monopolists. Certainly they have not done so in the past. But, besides counting on their goodwill, consumers could also rely upon the impact of certain countervailing forces over which their governments have some control: transitional energy subsidies, federal regulation of imports and exports to alter market conditions, and finally, gas and oil from federal reserves which will soon command an increasing proportion of the market. Energy prices will rise, but as I have tried to suggest here, not uncontrollably, and not necessarily to world levels. Alberta, Saskatchewan and British Columbia will get richer. That these provinces are already well off is no argument against their being better off. Moreover, reports of the impact of increased prices on eastern industry are greatly exaggerated.[46]

There might be other second-order advantages from this federal withdrawal from the energy field. Conflict with Ottawa has served to unite Albertans against the rest of the world. A solid regiment of Tories is sent down to Parliament to protest; one party, presenting itself as the guardian of the provincial patrimony against the federal wolf, completely dominates the provincial legislature, continuing the tradition of a quasi-party system in Alberta. Until the external threat is removed, the monolith will probably remain.

Federal-provincial conflict diminishes the possibility of genuine party competition.[47] In short, democracy is unlikely to return to Alberta until its citizens are free to disagree among themselves over the disposition of resource spoils, social and economic policies, and all the other issues that animate urban, industrial people.

Even after this retreat from positions taken in the 1970s, there will still be plenty of scope for federal ambition in the energy field. PetroCan will still require care and feeding, as will Panarctic, Syncrude, and Eldorado. Frontier pipelines will require careful planning and will probably also need public funding. The federal government will also be required to play a more active role either directly or through its Crown corporation in the international market. These are all important and demanding functions. Moreover, as Judith Maxwell has argued, all these tasks can be performed by the federal government with its existing powers.[48]

As I said at the beginning, we probably can't have a national energy policy—because the provinces have most of the jurisdiction—and we probably don't need one anyway—because energy forecasting cannot cope with rapid change, and because the provinces have the competence to generate and administer energy strategies of their own. Under the circumstances there is something to be said for policy pluralism, perhaps even competition. We will have to get along without a national energy policy just as we manage to get by without a national education policy, national professional licensing, or national price uniformity in most other important things, such as housing, for example. This is a federal country. It works best when jurisdictional boundaries are respected, not assailed. A retreat from centralized planning in the energy sphere might bring partial peace to one of the most refractory federal-provincial disputes. At present Alberta's Petroleum Marketing Commission is pitted against Ottawa's Petroleum Administration Act. Ultimately the Supreme Court may have to decide which takes precedence. Surely politicians, not judges, ought to settle issues as important as this.

III

In suggesting a decentralization of control over energy I am not unmindful of one of its unsettling consequences: the impact of higher provincial resource revenues upon federal finance. For that reason I qualified my proposal at the outset with the recommendation that the federal government withdraw from this field *for a consideration.*

Higher energy prices would swell provincial revenues accordingly. This in turn would wreck one of the most valuable federal institutions, the equalization scheme. For a generation the federal government has been making payments to provinces whose per-capita revenues are below the national average. Thus rich provinces are taxed to allow fiscally poor provinces to enjoy services of high quality without having to carry an excessive tax burden. Equalization is one of the wonders of our federal system, something that Canada has invented in the interests of equity, which must be preserved at all costs.[49] It also works. Since 1967 as a result of these fiscal transfers provincial per-capita incomes have been converging.[50]

Professor Thomas Courchene delivered a paper at the 1975 Victoria conference outlining the equalization implications of several price levels for oil and gas. Very briefly, the more Alberta and Saskatchewan receive for their resources—which cannot be taxed by Ottawa—the greater the difference between the have and the have-not provinces, and, therefore, the larger the federal compensation payout under the equalization formula.[51] Since 1975 energy prices have risen even more than Courchene's most extreme example and the Fiscal Arrangements Act, the equalization system, has been renegotiated. The federal government escaped from this uncomfortable position simply by excluding certain kinds of provincial revenue in whole or in part from the equalization calculation. Now provincial per-capita tax revenues are adjusted as if the western provinces were not receiving windfall resource revenues.[52] However skilful the sidestepping manoeuvre, it misses the point—equalization. It protects the federal budget and minimizes the deficit, but it does so at the expense of what has become one of the essential elements of our modern federal system.

Perhaps the federal government could bargain its way out of the energy field and return for a new equalization scheme which would involve the provinces as direct contributors. Equalization is defined as deviation from a national average. The amount fiscally rich provinces have exactly equals the amount poor provinces lack. Much of the present distortion stems from the exaggerated energy-related incomes of the western provinces. The higher the price of oil and gas, the greater the inter-provincial differential, the higher the pile of cash in the Alberta Heritage Fund. I suggest that fiscally rich provinces should contribute directly fifty per cent of the sum required for genuine equalization out of their own revenues. This would assist in recycling Canada's petro-dollars. It would come from money Canadians have paid for oil and gas. It would help maintain the principle of equalization in the greatly altered circumstances created by higher energy prices. Such a scheme might also curb the avarice of the energy-producing provinces somewhat, as approximately half of what comes in from higher prices would flow out again in equalization payments. Since some of the provinces have grown rich from natural resources sold to the rest of the country, there seems to be no reason for the federal government to continue to carry the responsibility for equalization alone.[53]

Why shouldn't the provinces pay a hundred per cent of equalizing per-capita provincial revenues? Why should the federal government still pay half? The answer in part is that we have entered an era when becoming a fiscally poor province is in some measure a statistical illusion. Ontario is at present a have-not province. But of course Ontario is very rich, as is Quebec, and both should be required to pay through federal taxes the sums needed to bring other provincial governments up to their level. Similarly, the federal government will soon be earning income of its own from frontier and offshore resources. When the Fiscal Arrangements Act comes up for renegotiation in 1982, there should still be a place for the federal government in the equalization program. Obviously, if the federal government were to involve the provinces directly, it would have to bargain. To get one must give. I suggest that the federal government use its relatively recently assumed energy responsibility as a counter in these discussions.

Thus, I conclude this review of a generation's speculation about and experience with the energy question, and the difficulties standing in the way of a national energy policy, with the suggestion that the federal government should trade its disputed jurisdiction in return for provincial contributions to the equalization scheme. This would close the circle. Energy revenues could be used to help refinance Confederation. Giving the provinces clearer control over energy policy could mark the beginning of 'Operation Disentanglement'—a reduction in the number of areas of shared jurisdiction and therefore deadlock—on whose immediate urgency Professors Cairns and Smiley have commented.[54] That seems to me to be something we could possibly have and definitely do need.

NOTES

1. Alan C. Cairns, 'The Other Crisis of Canadian Federalism', *Canadian Public Administration*, 22 (1979), pp. 175-95.
2. Hon. Mr Justice W. F. Carroll, Mr Angus J. Morrison, Hon. Mr Justice C. C. McLaurin, *Report of the Royal Commission on Coal, 1946* (Ottawa, 1947), p. 380.
3. *Ibid.*, pp. 395-6, 397, 400, 403, 579.
4. John Davis, *Canadian Energy Prospects* (Ottawa, 1957), pp. 30-2, 367-8. Interestingly the Davis study, undertaken during the height of the shift from coal to oil, overestimated the hegemony of petroleum. Recalculations done by economists at the Department of Energy, Mines, and Resources in the early 1970s reduced the importance of oil somewhat and enhanced the contribution of hydroelectricity. See EMR, *An Energy Policy For Canada: Phase 1* (Ottawa, 1973), vol. 1, p. 32.

Primary Energy Consumption
(percentages)

	1945		1955	
	Davis	EMR	Davis	EMR
Oil	21.2	18.5	49.1	38.0
Gas	2.7	2.3	5.9	4.6
Coal	57.3	51.5	31.4	28.7
Hydro	7.0	17.2	8.5	23.9
Wood	11.8	10.5	5.0	4.8
	100.0	100.0	100.0	100.0

5. For example, E. Ayres and C. A. Scarlott, *Energy Sources—the Wealth of the World* (New York, 1952); J. Dewhurst et al., *America's Needs and Resources* (New York, 1955); S. H. Schurr, B. C. Netschert, et al., *Energy in the American Economy,*

1850-1975 (Baltimore, 1960), and the President's Materials Policy Commission, *Resources for Freedom* (Washington, 1952) 5 vols.

6. Davis, *Canadian Energy Prospects*, pp. 67-8.

7. *Ibid.*, pp. 331-5.

8. Royal Commission on Canada's Economic Prospects, *Preliminary Report* (Ottawa, 1956), pp. 52-4.

9. Royal Commission on Canada's Economic Prospects, *Final Report* (Ottawa, 1957), pp. 123, 126-7. For background to the work of the Commission see Denis Smith, *Gentle Patriot* (Edmonton, 1973), pp. 31-50; Walter Gordon, *A Political Memoir* (Toronto, 1977), pp. 59-69.

10. Royal Commission on Energy, *First Report* (Ottawa, 1958); *Second Report* (Ottawa, 1959).

11. One Commissioner who was most certainly not sympathetic to the case of the western oilmen was the prairie economist George Britnell, who wrote a blistering minority report rejecting the nationalist arguments in favour of protection, from an orthodox free-trade point of view. See the *Second Report*, pp. 147-54. For a discussion of the National Oil Policy debate from the perspective of Robert Brown and Home Oil, see Philip Smith's fine company history, *The Treasure-Seekers: The Men Who Built Home Oil* (Toronto, 1978), pp. 186-208.

12. J. G. Debanné, 'Oil and Canadian Policy', in E. W. Erickson and L. Waverman, eds, *The Energy Question*, vol. 2 (Toronto, 1974), pp. 125-47; François Bregha, 'Canada's Natural Gas Industry', in J. Laxer, ed., *The Big Tough Expensive Job* (Toronto, 1976), pp. 63-94; *An Energy Policy For Canada: Phase 1*, vol. 2, pp. 335-6; A. R. Lucas, 'The National Energy Board', in G. B. Doern, ed., *The Regulatory Process in Canada* (Toronto, 1978), pp. 259-313.

13. For details on Canada's rising energy requirements in the 1960s, see EMR. *An Energy Policy For Canada: Phase 1*, vol. I, pp. 32-51; see also W. B. Friedenberg, *Energy In Canada: Review and Outlook to 1995* (Calgary, 1979), pp. 3-22. For the growth of the oil and gas industry during this period see Earle Gray, *The Great Canadian Oil Patch* (Toronto, 1970).

14. For Canadian energy use in an international perspective see J. Darmstadter, J. Dunkerley, and J. Alterman, *How Industrial Societies Use Energy: A Comparative Analysis* (Baltimore, 1977) and Z. C. Slagorsky's updated review, *Energy Use in Canada in Comparison with Other Countries* (Calgary, 1979).

15. National Energy Board, *Energy Supply and Demand in Canada and Export Demand for Canadian Energy 1966 to 1990* (Ottawa, 1969), pp. 47-64, which provided the information for approving the export of 6,295 bcf of natural gas in August 1970. See National Energy Board, *Report to the Governor in Council in the Matter of the Applications under the National Energy Board Act* (Ottawa, 1970).

16. J. G. Debanné, 'Oil and Canadian Policy', sets the background; for criticism of this period of Canadian-American energy relations see J. Laxer, ed., *The Big Tough Expensive Job*, especially the essays by Mel Hurtig and François Bregha, and J. Laxer, *The Energy Poker Game* (Toronto, 1970).

17. On falling reserves see Economic Council of Canada, *Eleventh Annual Review: Economic Targets and Social Indicators* (Ottawa, 1974) p. 117; Friedenberg, *Energy in Canada*, pp. 58, 61.

18. The best review of the oil crisis from a Canadian perspective is John Richards

and Larry Pratt, *Prairie Capitalism: Power and Influence in the New West* (Toronto, 1979), pp. 217-23; see also E. W. Erickson and Leonard Waverman, *The Energy Question*, vol. 1 (Toronto, 1974).

19. See for example Ontario Advisory Committee on Energy, *Energy in Ontario*, 2 vols (Toronto, 1972), and criticism in the Royal Commission on Electric Power Planning, *Interim Report: A Race Against Time* (Toronto, 1978), pp. 11-23.

20. Energy, Mines, and Resources, *An Energy Policy For Canada: Phase 1*, vol. 1, p. 104.

21. There is a convenient chronology of events in Energy, Mines, and Resources, *An Energy Strategy For Canada* (Ottawa, 1976), pp. 152-5; for a concise and comprehensive analysis of energy issues in the seventies see John F. Helliwell's bristling account, 'Canadian Energy Policy', in *Annual Review of Energy* (Palo Alto, 1979) pp. 175-229.

22. Economic Council of Canada, *Eleventh Annual Review: Economic Targets and Social Indicators* [1974], pp. 113-42; *Twelfth Annual Review: Options For Growth* [1975], pp. 19, 127-34; Judith Maxwell, *Energy Policy Challenges* (Montreal, 1974), Judith Maxwell, ed., C. D. Howe Research Institute, *Policy Review and Outlook, 1978* (Montreal, 1978), pp. 36-7.

23. For the furnace as man's natural enemy, see Robertson Davies, *The Diary of Samuel Marchbanks* (Toronto, 1947)—especially the entries for winter. See also the more pessimistic National Energy Board Reports, *Canadian Natural Gas Supply and Requirements* (Ottawa, 1975), *Canadian Oil Supply and Requirements* (Ottawa, 1975).

24. James E. Gander and Fred W. Belair, *Energy Futures For Canadians* (Ottawa, 1978), pp. 8, 11, 23, 26, 63, 97-8, 107, 128.

25. T. L. Powrie and W. D. Gainer, *Canadian Policy Toward Trade in Crude Oil and Natural Gas* (Ottawa, 1976), p. 113; T. L. Powrie, *Energy Policy and the Balance of Payments: An Outline of the Issues* (Calgary, 1979), p. 34.

26. Canadian Energy Research Institute, *Potential Markets For Thermal Coal in Canada, 1978-2000* (Calgary, 1979); R. L. Gordon, *Coal and Canada—U.S. Energy Relations* (Montreal, 1976).

27. Powrie, *Energy Policy And The Balance of Payments*; *Globe and Mail*, 21 and 26 Feb. 1980.

28. *Financial Post*, 9 Feb. 1980, Electric Power Report; Ontario Hydro Press Release, 16 Jan. 1980; *Toronto Star*, 15 Feb. 1980; *Globe and Mail*, 19 Feb. 1980.

29. Friedenberg, *Energy in Canada*, p. 59; Powrie, *Energy Policy and the Balance of Payments*, p. 41.

30. For the view from the other side of the border, see Melvin A. Conant and Associates, *The Western Hemispheric Energy System* (Washington, 1979), p. 51.

31. Gander and Belair, *Energy Futures For Canadians*, p. 111.

32. See the 1974 map accompanying the 1979 essay by Ian McDougall, 'Energy Natural Resources and the Economics of Federalism: National Harmony or Continental Hegemony', in E. J. Feldman and N. Nevitte, eds, *The Future of North America: Canada, the United States and Quebec Nationalism* (Cambridge, 1979), p. 201, which marks the whole eastern seaboard with a black x signifying 'presently insignificant finds'.

33. *Fortune*, 19 Nov. 1979; *Financial Post*, 1 Mar. 1970; *Globe and Mail*, 26 Mar. 1980.

34. Richard B. Mancke, *Squeaking By: U.S. Energy Policy Since the Embargo* (New York, 1976), p. 20.

35. *An Energy Policy For Canada: Phase 1*, vol. 1, p. 31.

36. McDougall, 'Energy, Natural Resources, Economics of Federalism'; A. M. Moore, 'The Concept of a Nation and Entitlements to Economic Rents', in A. Scott, ed., *National Resource Revenues: A Test of Federalism* (Vancouver, 1976), pp. 240-5.

37. Gander and Belair, *Energy Futures For Canadians*, p. 91.

38. Donald Smiley, 'The Political Context of Resource Development in Canada', in Scott, *Natural Resource Revenues*, pp. 71-2.

39. Andrée Lajoie, *Le Pouvoir déclaratoire du parlement: augmentation discrétionnaire de la compétence fédérale au Canada* (Montreal, 1969).

40. For commentary on the complex CIGOL *vs.* the Government of Saskatchewan case and decision see Richards and Pratt, *Prairie Capitalism*, pp. 294-301. For other views on the way in which the federal government might expand its jurisdiction see McDougall, 'Energy, Natural Resources, Economics of Federalism', and W. R. Lederman, 'The Constitution: A Basis For Bargaining', in Scott, *Natural Resource Revenues*, pp. 52-60.

41. British Columbia Energy Commission, *British Columbia's Energy Outlook 1976-1991* (Victoria, 1976); Ontario Advisory Committee on Energy, *Energy in Ontario* (Toronto, 1973); Direction générale de l'énergie, *L'Énergie au Québec* (Quebec, 1977), 3 vols, for three examples.

42. Slagorsky, *Energy Use in Canada in Comparison with Other Countries*.

43. A better case can be made for equalizing electricity rates than the price of oil. For interprovincial comparisons of electricity costs see *Financial Post*, 10 Nov. 1979. For insight into how muddled federal-provincial negotiations can get in energy-related matters see Neil Swainson, *Conflict Over the Columbia* (Montreal, 1979).

44. John Helliwell and Gerry May, 'Taxes, Royalties and Equity Participation as Alternative Methods of Dividing Resource Revenues: The Syncrude Case', in Scott, *Natural Resource Revenues*, pp. 153-80.

45. See Christopher Armstrong, *The Politics of Federalism* (forthcoming).

46. A. P. Ellison, *The Effects of Rising Energy Costs on Canadian Industries* (Calgary, 1979), and the *Globe and Mail*, 23 Feb. 1980.

47. For a retooled version of C. B. Macpherson's *Democracy in Alberta* (Toronto, 1953), see T. J. Lévesque and K. H. Norris, 'Overwhelming Majorities in the Legislature of Alberta', *Canadian Journal of Political Science*, XII (1979), pp. 451-70.

48. Scott, *Natural Resource Revenues*, pp. 181-4.

49. *Ibid.*, p. 68.

50. Economic Council of Canada, *Living Together* (Ottawa, 1977).

51. Thomas J. Courchene, 'Equalization Payments and Energy Royalties', in Scott, *Natural Resource Revenues*, pp. 74-107.

52. For commentary and analysis see Thomas J. Courchene, *Refinancing the Canadian Federation: A Survey of the 1977 Fiscal Arrangements Act* (Montreal, 1979).

53. For some variations on the theme of provincial participation in equalization

payments see Courchene, 'Equalization Payments and Energy Royalties', pp. 87-95. In a paper prepared about the same time as this one Professor Helliwell calculated the implications for the 1980s of three different oil and gas pricing policies upon provincial government revenues and the federal equalization program. On the basis of a sophisticated computation of relative cash flows he argued that the most effective method of restoring balance to the federal-provincial fiscal system would be the creation of an interprovincial revenue sharing fund. It would be in the interest of Alberta to pay people in other parts of Canada to stay where they are rather than suffer a flood of immigrants to sit under the oil wells and metaphorically clip coupons. See John F. Helliwell, 'The Distribution of Energy Revenues Within Canada: Functional or Factional Federalism?', University of British Columbia Economics Department, Resources Paper No. 48, February 1980. I am grateful to Professor Helliwell for providing me with copies of his papers bearing upon Canadian energy policy.

54. Cairns, 'The Other Crisis', pp. 194-5; Donald Smiley, 'Territorialism and Canadian Political Institutions', *Canadian Public Policy*, 3 (1977), pp. 449-57.

IV
Parliament, Parties
and Politicians

J. R. Mallory

PARLIAMENT IN THE EIGHTIES

The modern evolution of the Westminster system of government
has left Parliament with an ambiguous and little-understood role.
The most important day in the life of the back-bench member of
the House of Commons is the day when he is declared elected. That
is the day when we know for certain how many members each
party has, and therefore which party is going to govern the country. Thus even on that unique occasion the MP is simply part of the
scoreboard rather than one of the players on the field. Strict party
discipline means that once a government has a majority it is safe
until it terminates the life of the House of Commons and goes back
to the electorate. What happens in between is totally predictable
on every vote that takes place on the floor of the House. Gone (or
nearly gone) are the days when one could say with Walter Bagehot
that the House is a permanent electoral chamber which can create
or destroy a government when it chooses to do so. When this
actually happens (as in December 1979) it is a cause of general
wonderment and simulated resentment that the House has
deprived the government of its mandate to govern for 'a full term'.

Walter Bagehot's *The English Constitution* was published in
1867—the year of Confederation. At that time Bagehot could say
that both the monarchy and the House of Lords were on the way to
becoming merely ceremonial or 'dignified' parts of the constitution, with the real power passing to the 'efficient' parts such as the
cabinet. Was the late Richard Crossman right in suggesting that
the House of Commons itself was well on the way to becoming
merely one of the 'dignified' parts of the constitution? Certainly
legislatures under the Westminster system—and ours are no

exception—have been much slower to adapt themselves to an effective role in twentieth-century government than have the cabinet and the bureaucracy. There is little that the average MP can do as an independent part of the system. His power has been transferred to the cabinet and the party leadership.

Why has this happened? In part it is because the House is sinking in public esteem and sometimes appears to be trying to live up to its unfavourable image. I suspect that the unenthusiastic and by no means accurate public view of Parliament has been reinforced by the work of some modern political scientists. In their desire to penetrate the reality of politics in a scientific way, they have preferred things that can be measured to things that respond only to intuitive judgement. Hence their infatuation with polls, which seek to understand what the public thinks and why it behaves politically the way it does. If the public's views can be found out by polling, then what is the use of a body of 'representative' people whose business is to interpret them? Even the study of Parliament itself suffers from the same fashionable activity. One studies things that can be measured, like votes, or seeks to quantify members' attitudes because it is by no means easy to measure the efficacy of what they do. It must now be common knowledge that the role of members of Parliament in the generation of 'inputs' is minimal—for policy is pre-digested in the bureaucracy and the cabinet—and its contribution to 'outputs' is purely formal. The House simply legitimates what somebody else has already given to it as a finished product. The House thus seems to be a sort of vermiform appendix on the political process.

A better understanding of the role of an elected member in the Westminster system would lead to a less harsh verdict, but even so every serious student of the parliamentary system agrees that the performance of the House of Commons and of provincial legislative chambers must be improved. In fact, they must improve if a proper balance is to be restored to our political institutions.

There is some evidence that this is already happening. Televised proceedings have done something to improve the image of the House, and to disclose that something interesting and important is happening there. The fact that the cameras have been turned on has encouraged a degree of decorum among members which was often lacking in the past. The only danger is that the whole production may become too boring to watch most of the time. This risk is enhanced by the present restriction which the House of Commons imposes on broadcasters by requiring them to focus on one talking head at a time, partly because the whips have carefully arranged to fill the seats with attentive-looking members within range of the cameras. Roving shots that would pick up interruptions or dozing members are strictly forbidden. In Quebec, where the cameras have more freedom and the debates are more widely available, the results have been striking. The telecasts have provoked significant audience interest and improved public awareness of the National Assembly.

Televising debates will not be enough in itself. However, television may do something to counteract general media coverage of parliamentary institutions, which focuses on personalities and tries to create confrontations, even when they do not exist, in order to make news. The public has to perceive what is happening and understand it well enough to know if it is important. Unfortunately, the worst problem is that the average newsman on the parliamentary beat knows far less about what is happening than you or I do because he does not have time to pursue a story in depth and seldom has enough knowledge to do it intelligently. Reporters on the sports pages usually have an uncertain grasp of language, but at least they do know a great deal about their subject-matter.

Several things are likely to happen in the eighties that will have important effects on the House of Commons in Ottawa, though we can only guess what they will be. One of which we may be reasonably certain is that the electoral system will have to be changed—a change which will affect the whole party system as well as the working lives of members. The change to which I am referring is a departure from the single-member first-past-the-post system which up to now has been deemed to be an essential part of our parliamentary system. Of itself it does not much matter that a political party often achieves a comfortable majority of seats without polling even fifty per cent of the vote. What is important is that political parties may poll a substantial number of votes in a particular region of the country and yet be denied any seats. Thus in February 1980 the Conservative representation in the whole of Quebec was reduced from three to one, while there is not a single Liberal member west of Winnipeg. Parties which for years have been unable to translate a substantial vote into seats are ready converts to electoral reform, but when they do get into power under the same set of rules they tend to forget their zeal to change the system. For the party managers prefer the devil they know to the devil they don't.

However, the worst aspect of the present system, as Alan Cairns, over ten years ago, was one of the first to point out, is that it negates one of the most important supposed roles of political parties: the brokerage role, which transcends the regional cleavages that are a constant threat to federal systems.[1] Cairns has argued that the present electoral system is actually dysfunctional in that it has created a situation in which the different parties have overwhelming strength in some regions, but no party is able to elect a significant number in all regions. To put the point somewhat differently, the Conservatives are not a part of the party system in Quebec, while the Liberals have almost vanished from sight in the West, where the contest is between the Conservatives and the NDP. A party in government, as Sir John A. Macdonald said in 1863, needs to retain the confidence of all the country if it is to govern with authority and full legitimacy. Many observers have concluded that the present situation suppresses the fact that regionally 'invisible' parties in fact poll a significant share of the vote in the areas where they are unable to turn these votes into seats.

For over seventy years there have been advocates of proportional representation to cure this problem. Mackenzie King, who once had this idea pressed on him by Lord Grey, dismissed the idea as 'faddist'. But the faddists persist. The western Progressives were strong enough to have the idea seriously considered, and it was their influence that led to its partial adoption in provincial elections in Manitoba and Alberta. Nevertheless, the idea failed to take hold for two reasons. As Kenneth McNaught has pointed out, minority parties are eager to press for electoral reform when their support is small, but when they gain strength and approach the reality of power they prefer the advantages that the existing system offers. The second reason is that we in Canada have a lingering suspicion of coalitions, and proportional representation would almost certainly make coalition governments inevitable.[2]

Nevertheless, the present electoral configuration has led to wider acceptance for the idea. The latest version is to retain the present system but to add to it an additional body of 'members at large', elected from each province in order to ensure adequate representation of minorities. A number of scholars have been attracted to the idea, and it has gained further respectability by being enshrined both in the Pépin-Robarts Report and in the recent Beige Paper of the Quebec Liberal Party.[3] A consensus is growing that the problem is critical and that electoral reform embodying partial proportional representation is the most effective way to deal with it. The timelag even for reforms that everybody agrees on is still considerable, for there is likely to be much anxious debate about details, both before and after legislation is prepared, and a major reform has to find a place on a very crowded legislative timetable. For example, the timelag for the present election-expenses law was about ten years, and the same was true of the establishment of non-partisan electoral-boundary commissions. Nevertheless the proposal can no longer be dismissed as a fad. We shall see it adopted in the eighties.

It is likely to achieve its object in making it again possible for the parties in the House of Commons to include significant representation from the whole country. But will it have important side-effects? Take the proposal of the Pépin-Robarts Task Force. It would add about sixty seats to the House of Commons which would be filled by 'candidates from ranked lists announced by the parties before the election, seats being awarded to parties on the basis of percentages of the popular vote.' It will be recalled that they also wished to abolish the Senate and replace it with a Federal Council representing the provincial governments. The additional members elected on this new system were intended in part to carry on the role hitherto played by the Senate in committee scrutiny of the executive. Members without constituency responsibilities, it was reasoned, would—like senators today—have more time for committee work.

Would things work out like this? These PR members, unable to get elected in the normal way, would still be party men. While they would strengthen the partisan role of undermanned parties in the House of Commons, there is no certainty that they would have strong inclinations to carry out politically unrewarding work in committees any more than present members have. Furthermore, I suspect that the other members, who derive much satisfaction as well as effectiveness from doing as much as they can for their constituencies, would tend to treat these members with well-modulated respect. The fact that some of the new members would have a new and easy route to the cabinet if they were in the government party would increase the tension between them and the 'constituency' members. It would, I suspect, have a tendency to undermine the club-like atmosphere that continues to underlie the House even when it is at its most hostile.

The House of Commons does a number of important and necessary things. One of its problems has been that its numbers have been insufficient to do them as effectively as it might. One of the most significant changes in the last ten years is the much greater extent to which the business of the House has been removed from the floor and put into committee. The committees now deal with practically all legislation (except financial legislation) as well as the annual review of the estimates, and from time to time undertake serious policy studies. As long as the size of the House was restricted under the old system to a ceiling of about 265, most of these things were done badly. There simply were not enough members to do the job, especially since governments now contain about thirty ministers, attended by as many as twenty-seven parliamentary secretaries. The committees have to have chairmen, and sometimes vice-chairmen, and the Speaker himself has three deputies. How many are left to man the committees? The Créditistes, when they had significant numbers in the House, hardly bothered with committees at all. They were too few to do much good anyway, and they found it electorally more useful to spend practically all of their time on constituency work. Furthermore, at any one time a fair number of members are ill; some are in fact lazy. The number of members who can be regarded as good committee men has been put by some estimates as low as sixty. One way to mitigate the problem might be to decrease the size of committees and also their number, but I suspect that this would have only limited effect.

I think myself that the most important thing is to increase the size of the House. This is now happening naturally as a result of the new representation system introduced by an amendment to the British North America Act in 1974. Under the new formula the House will have 282 members in the present decade and will probably rise to over 350 by the end of the century. Something like the Pépin-Robarts proposal would add about sixty more.

What will the effect of these changes be? A minor but not irrelevant consideration is the fact that the present chamber is close to its full capacity. Members' chairs and desks could not be made much smaller unless all members possessed the physical dimensions of the Hon. Stanley Knowles, or it might be possible to reduce the size of the galleries, probably at the Speaker's end of the chamber. In the end we shall probably have to settle for an entirely new chamber, or else adopt the British practice of undifferentiated benches and do away with seats and desks for individual members, which have been standard accommodation since colonial times.

Nevertheless I think that an increase in members is essential if the potential of committees is to be fully exploited. The present system could not function at all if the whips were not permitted to substitute at short notice without obtaining the consent of the House, which means that, while every committee has a small core of experienced members, on any given day perhaps half the members present have been brought in as last-minute substitutes. Officials appearing before committees dealing with the estimates find that very often questions answered at the last meeting are brought up again by members unaware of what had previously transpired. This is frustrating and inefficient. The only solution so far has been that adopted a couple of years ago by the Standing Committee on Labour, Manpower, and Immigration while it was engaged on a long and complex study of policy. An agreement was reached with the whips that there would be a continuing core of alternates so that the committee would always be made up of members familiar with the subject-matter. It is fairly clear, however, that if all committees did this it would be self-defeating, for there would not be nearly enough members to go around.

I should say that, sensible as it sounds, not everyone agrees on the serious need to enlarge the House. Two senior members of the House of Commons staff, who had better not be named, and who have had ample opportunity to see members at work, have told me that numbers will do no good because there are already too many idle members and that most of them do not have enough to do. I prefer to be less pessimistic.

The question of overload is, however, perhaps more than a lack of members to do a job that can be done. The Hon. Robert Stanfield has argued strongly that the whole process of government is overloaded.[4] Government now embraces so much of our lives that it has outrun the capacity to manage matters. 'If ministers have put themselves in an impossible position,' he says, 'consider the poor Member of Parliament. Parliament is not fitted for controlling the kind of all-pervasive government we have today.' He is not sure that we can restore a situation where the House of Commons can effectively supervise government, but if we can it will be necessary first to cut back on the role of government.

If, as seems possible, the time is coming when we can no longer expect the Senate to do the unglamorous jobs which the Commons has neither the time nor the inclination to do because they seem irrelevant to the party battle, we shall have to give the Commons even more facilities and hope that it will respond. There is no political payoff, and little pleasure, in reading through hundreds of orders in council to make sure that they comply with the law and common sense. Nor is there much to be gained politically from taking a hard look at very complicated but politically uninteresting bills. And without the Senate we should need a great many more royal commissions, task forces, and so forth—mounted at much greater expense and probably lacking in the considerable pool of wisdom and experience that exists unsung in the Senate.

In the everyday work of Parliament both senators and members of the Commons have a problem with information. In a sense the difficulty is more acute in the Commons, where few members survive for long periods, and members have less opportunity and leisure to become expert in many matters. We are frequently told that MPs are unable to do their jobs because information is withheld from them. This is often true. Governments, from the most influential minister down to the lowest bureaucrat, are naturally secretive. This is often necessary. Full discussion requires that the participants take extreme positions in arguing a question through in order to reach a solution, which is why negotiations in progress are unlikely to succeed if conducted in public. Neither ministers nor civil servants can afford to argue positions that would fatally compromise them if adopted in public, so that secrecy is a necessary part of the process. However, secrecy can be a convenient shield to cover up mistakes and those responsible for them. The Freedom of Information bill, which unfortunately died with the dissolution of the Thirty-first Parliament, would have gone a long way to achieving a better balance between necessary secrecy and greater openness in government. One only hopes that it will be revived. Gerald Baldwin was undoubtedly right in thinking that the only chance for this to happen is during the honeymoon period when a new government is freshly in office and as yet unaccustomed to the comforts of excessive secrecy. The results of the election of 18 February do not therefore give much ground for hope. There is still a great deal of secrecy about, and the 'need to know' principle does not seem to apply either to MPs or to ordinary citizens. But even if we could eradicate unnecessary secrecy, a much more serious problem would remain. The Member of Parliament today has far too much information to digest.

His routine reading matter is enormous. Hundreds of bills are tabled in each session and he will have to read and digest at least those that pertain to his special interests and the committees on which he may be sitting. The Main Estimates, which consist of 1,200 pages of figures and not very intelligible explanation, need perusal for the same reason. He is unlikely to read all of Hansard, but apart from correcting the 'blues' of his own speeches, he will need to read the speeches in debates in which he is interested— particularly since he was probably absent from the House on committee or other business when they were delivered. Politicians are avid newspaper readers, and newspapers are more entertaining to read than official documents. The member's daily volume of constituency mail will itself be substantial, and in most cases will require a good deal of time on the telephone before it can be answered. Some of his mornings will be taken up in caucus and other meetings; the House and its committees are likely to claim the rest. What resources has he got to cope with all of these things?

Within the last decade or so things have changed for the better. I can remember when backbench members usually shared an office and a typist with someone else. The conversion of first the West Block and later the Confederation Building has now largely solved the problem of office space. In addition, members' staff resources have been improved immeasurably in recent years. They now have funds to provide themselves with staff both in the House and in their constituencies, with the possibility of increasing one at the expense of the other within certain limits. At the beginning of 1977 nearly two hundred members had office staff of three people in Ottawa; others had fewer, but presumably more in their constituencies.[5] One would guess that the great bulk of staff time is in fact devoted to constituency business. It may be significant that when members were offered a policy assistant in place of one of the office positions, only one member chose to accept. Mr Fraser thought that, on the whole, staff resources for constituency matters (the ombudsman role) were adequate, but that active members with heavy committee assignments had some cause to complain.

There are, of course, additional resources which members can and do use. Many are able to make use of parliamentary interns who, however inexperienced in the nuances of parliamentary life, are nevertheless eager and trained in the art of speedily assimilating and digesting complex material. Then there are the caucus research staffs. There seems to be a low opinion of their value among the staff of the House itself, and at least in the early stages there were serious difficulties in relating their work to the needs of caucus spokesmen in the House and on committees.[6] However, they have added substantially to the resources of Opposition parties, whether or not they are always used to the best advantage. Finally, there is the Parliamentary Library itself, which is no longer merely the best public library in Ottawa, in which a bookish member could find ample food for serious or light reading. It now has a research staff which will go well beyond merely assembling material to the point of writing draft speeches appropriately 'slanted'. The tradition of neutrality is preserved by the willingness of the staff to do the same for all parties. These are not inconsiderable resources and we can be sure that they will increase, probably on the same scale, over the next decade.

One of the principal causes of complaint is that, while individual members and caucuses now have considerable support services, committees generally have none. This is not completely true, since the Public Accounts Committee gets considerable support from the Auditor-General, and the Joint Committee on Statutory Instruments has its own counsel and a modest staff. Other committees, particularly when they are engaged in the study of white or green papers, may occasionally be given staffs *ad hoc*.

The argument has been made that committees should have staffs of their own, like American congressional committees. In the American system committees play a central role as a sort of counter-executive in legislation and the administration through the control of funding. If our committees assumed that role it would wholly alter the nature of our parliamentary system, which is based on executive dominance. Under responsible government it is the cabinet that governs and it is not the business of Parliament to try and govern in its place. The majority in the House of Commons conceives its business to be to support the government, while the minority Opposition complains, publicizes grievances, and develops alternative policies with which it hopes to win the next election.

How far would the work of the House be enhanced by committee staffs? Peter Dobell is I think right to be cautious. Certain kinds of committees, such as those engaged in a serious and lengthy enquiry, do need the support of expert staff. But, says Dobell, 'I disagree with the priority usually given to the provision of committee staffs for two reasons. First, until other deficiencies are overcome, the provision of permanent committee staff would be costly, ineffective and sometimes soul-destroying for the persons hired. Second, committees already have considerable access to staff resources.'[7] Some committees, whose primary role is supervision of the executive, already have appropriate staff resources, as is the case with Public Accounts and Statutory Instruments. Staffs retained *ad hoc* come late in the day, are not always familiar with parliamentary requirements, and do not play a clear role. Are they only at the service of the chairman, available to any committee member who wants them, or should some of them be attached to each party in the committee? The line between purely technical questions, on which the experts are presumed to be knowledgeable, and 'political' questions is often blurred. Experts employed under contract are often unfamiliar with how Parliament works, while a permanent pool would be expensive but unworkable. Also most committees have a highly variable work load, and the kind of experts needed varies greatly from time to time. The existence of a large body of available consultants presents the danger that these firms would be more interested in selling their services and making work than in assisting members. Furthermore, permanent committee staffs are open to the objection that they would tend to usurp the role of the members themselves.

The major transformation in the House of Commons in the seventies was to transfer much of the real and important work of members off the floor of the House and into the committee rooms. This work is valuable and only minor changes would make it much more effective than it is. However, there is still important work that must be done on the floor of the House. Even here fairly small but important changes would improve matters. A number of useful improvements were suggested by the late Conservative government's Position Paper on the Reform of Parliament. These included reducing the time of speeches in the House from the present forty minutes to twenty; a positive and negative resolution procedure to enhance the capacity of the House to keep a watchful eye on delegated legislation; and a reduction in the number of Allotted Days from twenty-five to twenty. There were also some useful suggestions to improve the work of committees by reducing their size and improving their effectiveness in other ways. It is to be hoped that these proposals will now be revived in the new parliament. One of them would have the approbation of Mitchell Sharp, who regarded Allotted Days as largely a waste of time, and who thought matters could be improved by bringing back some departmental estimates onto the floor of the House on Allotted Days.[8]

Other proposals, which have been made by Professor John Stewart, would include the drastic curtailment of second-reading debates, as is now done at Westminster. The second-reading debate is essentially intended to discuss the principle of a bill, and allowing this debate to drag on is a very imperfect way of giving closer attention to its details which can be dealt with more profitably at a later stage. Similarly it might be advantageous to send a contentious bill straight to committee after first reading, as is frequently done in the National Assembly in Quebec. The advantage of this is that the government, before allowing itself to be irretrievably committed to the bill as it stands, can be more receptive to modification in its details.[9]

What is needed is a House, or, to be realistic, an opposition adequately equipped to make effective criticism. The Lambert commission argued that neither Parliament nor the public now has adequate information to understand government policy.[10] The

Estimates, which are now about the only way that Parliament can get at what policy is, are intelligible only to accountants and do not disclose what the objectives of government programs are, whether these objectives have been achieved, or exactly who is responsible for carrying them out. The Commission have made a number of recommendations to improve these matters. Perhaps their key recommendation is that Parliament should annually debate the general fiscal plan of the government over the next five years. Then we should be able to know not only where the government is going, but whether it knows where it is going. The Commission also suggested improvements in the organization of the bureaucracy which would, without undermining the sacred doctrine of ultimate ministerial responsibility, make it more feasible for senior officials to be held accountable for their actions. All this is to the good. Undoubtedly parliaments in the eighties will be able to build on reforms of the past twenty years in order to strengthen their role in the system.

In our efforts to 'improve' the work of the House of Commons we must never lose sight of the fact that it is a political body made up of political parties whose *raison d'être* is to win the electoral battle and become the government of the country. No activity, no matter how worthy, which does not accord with this primary objective is likely to be embraced by the House. Members of Parliament are ambitious politicians who do best what they like to do and find most rewarding. If they are to be successful they must contrive to be elected, and the next election is never far from their minds. They are good party men who know that it is necessary to vote in the House when the division bells ring, and to spend a great deal of time just being a party presence in committee or on the floor of the House. Most of the time these are not very rewarding experiences.

If routine parliamentary duties are often dull and frustrating, other sources of satisfaction can be found in the daily work of the member of Parliament. Much of his time is spent in dealing with the problems of his constituents. A great many of these are beyond his power to deal with, but in a large number of cases he can help by telephoning an insensitive department or by raising the problem in the House. When he is able to solve a constituent's problem he is bound to feel a sense of satisfaction and achievement. He also knows that being a good constituency man is one of the best ways of retaining the continued support of the voters. No wonder that most members seem to have a 'case-work' syndrome, and that they devote the maximum amount of their still meagre staff resources to the task. As citizens whose lives are more and more entangled with government rules, we should be grateful that they do.

But what has become of the grander role of Parliament if a member is reduced to being either a foot-soldier in a party machine or an ombudsman? Surely there is more to Parliament than that— and of course there ought to be. The day-to-day answerability of ministers on the floor of the House of Commons does much to mitigate the arrogance of power, but this process must be informed and effective if it is to work. The important task of parliamentary reform is to strengthen the House as an institution. There are some kinds of reform which are unlikely to strengthen its role as a counterpoise to government. One of these is the suggestion that there be a much greater opportunity to pass private members' bills, even though it might make life more interesting for backbenchers. This is one of the matters which it was understood that the Conservatives were considering when they were elected in 1979.

The suggestion was great news for the gun lobby, the advocates of the restoration of capital punishment, and the anti-abortionists, all of whom seemed to think that politicians are too frightened of offending large and vocal groups of voters to risk what appear to be unpopular stands. However, when the reform proposals came down it was clear that the government was being cautious. They were willing to give more time for full debate of private members' business instead of allowing it to be automatically 'talked out'. The proposed changes would have allowed such business to be discussed more fully and more easily brought to a vote, but there would be time for a great deal less of such business. In this I think they were wise. Most important decisions involve careful balancing of a great many conflicting and delicate pressures, and only a responsible government has both the information and the strength to take such decisions. Governments are, of course, often wrong, but differences of this sort are what party politics is intended to deal with.

Changes in the rules and practices of the House can make it a more effective body. However, rule changes in themselves will accomplish little unless members can employ them effectively. This is partly a question of attitudes and partly a question of the capacity of members to do the job. In the society of the eighties not only are more people going to be better educated, but far more of them will be familiar with the working life of large organizations. In the past the average member of Parliament was likely to possess neither the intellectual skills nor the managerial skills appropriate to his job. Unless he was a lawyer, trained to assimilate a brief quickly, he was not likely to be effective as a policy critic on a committee—and even lawyers are not always good at running up good briefs without assistance. Since members of Parliament had little or nothing in the way of staff, few of them developed the managerial skills to make the most of what resources there were. In the House of Commons in 1980 the successful member not only needs to be sufficiently educated to grasp a large number of complex issues quickly, but above all needs to make effective use of the considerable staff resources so that the information that is available is actually used. I think therefore that the new breed of parliamentarian of the eighties will need to master these skills. Improvement will come from an inevitable response to the needs of the job, rather than a response to elaborate proposals for reform cooked up by those of us on the outside. Democracy is not merely a matter of choosing our rulers, but also of keeping them accountable for their actions. Competing political parties create the organized strength to do these things, and the House of Commons is one of the essential means by which parties in a democracy operate.

NOTES

1. Alan C. Cairns, 'The Electoral System and the Party System in Canada, 1921-65', *Canadian Journal of Political Science*. 1, 1 (March 1968) p. 62.
2. 'History and Perception in Politics' in J.H. Redekop, *Approaches to Canadian Politics* (Toronto, 1979), p. 110.
3. The Task Force on Canadian Unity, *A Future Together* (Ottawa, 1979), pp. 104-6; The Constitutional Committee of the Quebec Liberal Party, *A New Canadian Federalism* (Montreal, 1980), p. 46.
4. W.A.W. Neilson and J.C. MacPherson, *The Legislative Process in Canada* (Montreal, 1978), p. 44.

5. Alistair Fraser, 'Legislators and their Staffs', paper presented to the Second Conference on Legislative Studies, Simon Fraser University, February 1979.

6. See Edwin R. Black, 'Opposition Research: Some Theories and Practice', *Canadian Public Administration*, 15, 1 (Spring 1972), pp. 24-41.

7. 'Committee Staff—What Else Is Needed?', paper presented to the Second Conference on Legislative Studies, Simon Fraser University, February 1979.

8. For the details of Mr Sharp's criticism see J.R. Mallory 'The Two Clerks: Parliamentary Discussion of the Role of the Privy Council Office', *Canadian Journal of Political Science*, 10, 1 (March 1977), p. 12. For a discussion of the aborted Conservative proposals see *Parliamentary Government*, 1, 2 (January 1980).

9. John B. Stewart, *The Canadian House of Commons: Procedure and Reform* (Montreal, 1977).

10. Royal Commission on Financial Management and Accountability, *Final Report* (Ottawa, 1979).

Denis Smith

POLITICAL PARTIES
AND THE SURVIVAL OF CANADA

I should like to take the title of this essay almost literally. If it is true—as I believe it is—that the maintenance of Confederation in something like its present form hangs in the balance in 1980, then what part have our political parties had in bringing us to that precarious stage, and what prospects do they offer for taking us through the present crisis to a state of renewed or fresh constitutional equilibrium?

The crisis is not quite literally a crisis of physical survival. We do not face the imminent possibility that Canada and its citizens will suddenly disappear from the face of the earth—unless there is a nuclear holocaust. (That eventuality lies beyond the influence of Canadian political parties, so that there is not much to be gained from considering their attitudes to it: undoubtedly they're agin it, and that's that.) What we do face is the prospect that the survival of Canada in its present constitutional shape, as a federation of ten provinces whose relationships are formally governed by the terms of the British North America Act, may be at stake. The twenty-four million people who occupy the territory called Canada, or most of them, seem likely to go on living in political association; the question is whether it will be much the same association as at present, or whether it is destined to change substantially in character. The activity of the parties in creating and resolving that crisis of constitutional forms is an urgent matter for consideration.

There are thoughtful Canadians, of course, who deny that we face a constitutional crisis at all. I have talked to several federal politicians in the past two years who have argued that the constitutional alarums and excursions in Canada since 1960 have been nothing more serious than fashionable games; that those who press hardest for constitutional change do not in fact want to achieve it; and that the rest of us need only wait patiently or complacently until the constitutional flurries die away, when we will be able to return to the enjoyment of our blessings under the federal constitution of 1867. I have heard other Canadians argue, slightly differently, that there may indeed be a crisis, in the sense that some provinces or regions strongly challenge the rules and practices of the federal system as it exists; but that the ways of Canadian politics just do not allow for the satisfaction of such basic challenges to the system. This kind of diagnosis usually calls not only for patience or complacency in working out the discontent, but for more active and defiant traits: the courage to hold on firmly, or the will to resist. This attitude is certainly less soft-headed than the first; it may even involve a shrewd assessment of how much change the Canadian political system can normally accommodate in an orderly way; but I suspect that it also underestimates the determination of those who advocate major constitutional change. It therefore stops short of facing the hardest dilemma: if the system can't take much orderly change, and if the advocates of change have the power and the determination to press their claims nonetheless, what kind of political ingenuity will be needed to avert political breakdown? (The answer to that question could be that none is available.)

In contrast to such views, I judge that there is a constitutional crisis in Canada which time alone will not dissipate, which is worsening and approaching its climax, yet which is still open to political resolution. Given the recent historical record, however, the likelihood of a tolerable political settlement must appear slight. Canadian political parties have made a less than satisfactory contribution to that record; but they have also been the victims of circumstances. While they might have done many small things—and thus averted some consequences of the crisis—I am not sure that they could, realistically, have done any big thing sufficient to avert the crisis itself. It is a crisis of world-historical scale, while they are only weak and mortal institutions.

Here is how the Pépin-Roberts Task Force on Canadian Unity defines the challenge to Canadian political survival:

While we take the election of the Parti Québécois as our point of departure, we do not regard that event, or any single federal election, or the pending Quebec referendum as defining the sense and substance of the issues the Task Force must tackle. Whether the referendum is 'won' or 'lost', the underlying problems will remain and will have to be confronted. We believe that such events as these should be taken to *symbolize* the political crisis Canada is facing, rather than to *constitute* it. The political crisis which has led to such occurrences displays historical roots which are much deeper and dimensions which are broader than any single event can comprehend, and its rhythms of development are slower and more inexorable than a single election or referendum would suggest....

Since the early 1960s ... considerable efforts at reform have been made in Quebec, in the other provinces, and in Ottawa. Yet more than a decade after the warning of the B & B Commission about a national crisis, the country has moved to an even graver and more critical stage in its history, symbolized by the election of a secessionist government in Quebec....

The crisis which the country faces today is not one of Quebec or of French Canada only: it is a crisis of Confederation itself. In this sense, the challenge to the country differs from that of a decade ago and must be considered in much wider terms. To the fundamental challenge of Canadian duality must now be added the other important challenge of Canadian regionalism....

Canadians now find themselves in a situation quite unlike any they have faced before. While we have had major crises in the past, this one is qualitatively different. The diverse elements ... have converged at one point in time and, partly as a result of this convergence, the rather rough-and-ready consensus which once ensured the reasonably effective governing of the country is at the point of breaking down.[1]

That analysis seems to me to be neither alarmist nor exaggerated, but rather a calm and sober statement of the truth.

It is not too difficult in retrospect to understand why the consensus has broken down. Above all, what gave Canada its confidence and its expansive prospects in the nineteenth century was the existence of the British Empire. The Empire was both a moral and a material force in the world, just reaching its apogee: elevated, in the minds of the smug and adventurous Englishmen and Scotsmen who made and managed it, to the very heights of the earthly paradise. There was nothing better in the world; there had been nothing better in the world. In the Empire the sun never set; material progress never ceased; English liberty and parliamentary institutions were to bring men as close to moral perfection as anyone would care to be. (And the Church of England was there when necessary to tolerate the lapses.) Within this great protective umbrella Canada came to birth in 1867. While Canadian politicians could foresee a gradual and benevolent evolution to autonomy within the Empire, the inspirational strength of the Empire, the certainty about values and institutions, appeared eternal. They remained eternal (with a few twinges of mortality at the time of the South African War) until 1918, and for many Canadians even (though in what was becoming more evidently a period of half-life) until 1945.

I think that the cohesive strength for Canadians of this imperial vision, implanted from without, cannot easily be overestimated during the first eighty years of confederation. After 1945 Britain's imperial power and will were gone. As the Empire faded away in the fifties and sixties, and as Britain turned inwards to agonize over her own domestic problems, English Canada lost one—perhaps the most profound—of her spiritual props. Some sense of the confusion and desperation that this loss entailed for British Canadians (a loss that most of the time could find no expression) was displayed in John Diefenbaker's futile objection to Britain's entry into the European Common Market, or in Donald Creighton's fulminations about the road not taken after 1945. Nothing replaced the loss of this source of transcendental assurance: not membership in the pallid Commonwealth; not the Department of External Affairs' earnest participation in United Nations good works; not half-integration into the American economy community; not the weakness and immaturity of domestic Canadian nationalism. And nothing that Canadian political parties could have done would have prevented this loss.

The second source of strength and self-confidence in Victorian and early twentieth-century Canada was the expansionist and centralist ambition of the commercial and political class, the financiers, railroad builders, manufacturers, and politicians of Montreal and southern Ontario who shaped the BNA Act and its continental purposes. These were men of large vision and presumption, spurred by the living example of the British empire and by the competitive challenge of the expanding American nation to the south to create their own continental empire within the broader framework of the British global empire. But their continental empire lacked any spiritual justification of its own: that was provided for it by the British element. The Dominion of Canada, on its own terms, found its nobility in railroads: the conquest and material development of a vast half-continent, the political and financial power at the centre that would accompany so audacious an achievement. Such a vision of development was plausible only in the age of technology; and, like the vision of Rhodes and Milner in southern Africa, it bore its own contradiction at its heart. The new communities of the West that joined or were created by the new federation to achieve its mercantilist purposes were not satisfied in their status of colonial subordination. From early in the twentieth century, the country grew familiar with the insistence of the Western provinces that they should somehow play a full and equal part in the political and economic life of the nation. Concessions were made; but it appeared by the early sixties that the central-Canadian bias of the federation—based as it was on a complex of institutional, geographical, and demographic conditions—could only be altered fundamentally by reforms that central Canada would be unwilling to contemplate and that the West was not yet ready to insist upon. The sense of dissatisfaction remained; and it was clear that, whatever the myth of Canadian unity that was transmitted to the outside world or accepted in Ottawa and Toronto, closer to the ground that unity was extremely fragile. The allegiance of the West was skeptical, and conditional upon the future adjustment of the political balance in its favour. The political parties of western Canada have been leading carriers of that skepticism since 1921.

With the confidence of Empire and the unquestioned predominance of central Canada already gone, two sets of events above all have thrown Canadian stability into doubt since 1960: the awakening of French-speaking Quebec to a confident sense of its national destiny, and the windfall accumulation of resource income in the West (and perhaps soon in Newfoundland too) which has followed from the actions of OPEC since 1973. These events, vigorously promoted and exploited by all the provincial political parties of Quebec (in the first case) and by the governing parties and their administrations in Saskatchewan, Alberta, and British Columbia (in the second case), have finally brought us to the constitutional crisis proclaimed by the Pépin-Robarts Task Force. The crisis involves more than a conflict of centre versus periphery; it involves, as well, the disintegration of the centre itself, resulting from the dramatic appearance in Quebec of a formerly hidden periphery, the Québécois nation. It is not obvious to me what resources of spirit and will, beyond the strength of political inertia and vested interest, the central government can now bring to the maintenance of its authority. Pépin-Robarts concluded that Ottawa's wisest course would be to concede the weakness of its historic position and take the initiative in negotiating a new Confederation settlement that would entrench the enhanced power and authority of Quebec and the Western provinces.

No government, anywhere, abandons power easily or by choice. Ottawa is no exception. In principle, the Trudeau government has insisted since 1968 that it does not have to, and should not do so. But its record in the fruitless rounds of constitutional discussion of the last twelve years hardly sustains its case: that record suggests instead that an unyielding defence of the federal power is untenable. Indeed, the unsatisfactory record of all three federal parties on the constitutional question must be taken, I believe, as strong evidence that the system within which they work has failed.

In the case of the Liberal Party, it is hardly accurate to describe its constitutional position as that of the party, or even of the cabinet. It is the position of Prime Minister Trudeau, his few political intimates, and his constitutional advisers in the bureaucracy. As George Radwanski notes in his recent political biography of the prime minister, the cabinet rarely influenced the government's constitutional stance after 1968;[2] nor did the party in its intermittent national gatherings. It is surely extraordinary, and the result of something more than Mr Trudeau's intellectual eminence, that the largest and most significant question before the country in the last decade (as the prime minister insisted during the 1979 campaign) has never in that time been the subject of serious debate in the governing party. This is not to say that some Liberals have not sought to bring the question into debate— Gordon Gibson of Vancouver is pre-eminent among them—but where has the effort gotten them? The party, in 1968, effectively delegated responsibility for dealing with the constitutional problem to its leader, and the country endorsed that delegation in the general election that followed. There was a sense, in those heady days, that Mr Trudeau was going to put Quebec in its place, renew

Canadian unity, and satisfy the aspirations of French-speaking Canadians all at once. Beyond belief in those bromides, the party and the country did not probe.

When the Trudeau government's idiosyncratic effort to achieve constitutional reform collapsed in the aftermath of the October Crisis and the Victoria Conference of June 1971, English-speaking Canada and the Liberal Party greeted the failure compacently and for five years shared the government's indifference to the constitutional question.

The election of the Parti Québécois government in November 1976 threw the federal government into panic, and English-speaking Canada into one of its sporadic bouts of confusion and alarm. The country's alarm lasted only a few months; it was soon dissipated by the demonstrated caution and competence of the new Quebec government. But the Trudeau government's panic lasted longer: it was institutionalized in a series of emergency projects ranging from the Canadian Unity Information Office to the Discovery Train to the increasingly elaborate celebration of Canada Day to a fresh round of constitutional conferences. One of the characteristics of the post-November federalist reaction, as in 1968, was that it took the form of a governmental, rather than a party, response. The Liberal Party did not enter into reflective analysis of the country's future. The Liberal government pre-empted the role, at least superficially, by treating the Parti Québécois challenge as a threat to the federal government's propagandist ingenuity rather than a serious challenge to its constitutional authority. The most that Ottawa wanted in the form of public participation in the debate after 1976 seemed to be sentimental declarations of allegiance to national unity. It apparently never occurred to anyone influential in the Liberal Party that it, *as a party*, had any responsibility to reassess the institutions of Canadian federalism.

The prospect of Quebec's independence was, understandably, too sensitive a subject for the Liberal Party to contemplate. Quebec was the basis of the party's hold on federal office, and it believed that hold to be permanent. No one questions the earth beneath one's feet.

Below the superficial efforts of propaganda, the federal government's more substantial response to the Parti Québécois appears, on close examination, to lack the coherence and determination of

its previous initiatives in the constitutional wars. The Parti Québécois victory has, I believe, destroyed the confidence of the Trudeau administration in its constitutional mission. It no longer has
a clear sense of purpose or a constitutional strategy. The government took four major steps after 1976 to deal with the Quebec
challenge:

(i) it renewed its attempts, through the federal-provincial conferences,
to reach agreement on a constitutional amending formula and a respect-
able package of substantive amendments;

(ii) in tandem with that effort it introduced, in June 1978, its own
constitutional bill, C-60, and set a three-year timetable for its complete
adoption;

(iii) it appointed the Task Force on Canadian Unity to buy time; and

(iv) it introduced a federal referendum bill designed to allow Ottawa to
counter a PQ referendum victory with a contradictory result of its own
manufacture, either within Quebec or across Canada.

By the spring of 1979 all these initiatives had collapsed. The
constitutional reforms that Ottawa discussed with the federal-
provincial conferences of October 1978 and February 1979, in spite
of their greater flexibility as compared with earlier federal proposals, proved unacceptable to the provinces. Bill C-60, a monument
of careless constitutional draftsmanship, was demolished as it
deserved to be in parliamentary committee over the summer of
1978 and was never proceeded with; the Pépin-Robarts Task Force,
when it reported in January 1979, showed its independence of the
prime minister by recommending an approach to constitutional
renewal profoundly subversive of Mr Trudeau's centralism; and
the federal referendum bill, which the prime minister insisted had
the highest priority, died on the order paper when Parliament was
dissolved at last by the prime minister's hand in March 1979. That
was not a record to inspire much confidence, and by the time of the
first 1979 dissolution more and more Canadians—including
Liberals—had judged that the emperor had no clothes. The prime
minister's insistence that the constitution was the issue of first
importance in the 1979 campaign struck no popular chords, I
think, largely because it was evident that he no longer had a
constitutional policy. As I wrote in *The Canadian Forum*, by then
he had only a growl.[3]

And where does the Liberal Party stand on the constitution now that it has returned so suddenly to power? Nowhere. The party never passed beyond the preliminaries in reassessing this or any other subject during its short term in opposition. The prime minister, abiding by the advice of his cynical advisers, neglected to mention the subject during the 1980 campaign; he was probably glad of that because he seemed to have nothing to say. The grand constitutional strategist of 1968 is in office once again, but this time without even the shreds of a policy.

There is much less to say about the constitutional positions of the federal Progressive Conservative Party and the NDP. The Conservatives, with a clear run of three years in opposition under a new leader from 1976 to 1979—a period of preparation for power— failed almost totally to consider and develop a general position on constitutional change. The party avoided any coherent response to the program of the Parti Québécois. It offered only a short-term, tactical alternative to the approach of the Trudeau government: opposition to the federal referendum bill on the ground, not that there shouldn't be one, but that it should be more narrowly drawn; a healthy skepticism toward Ottawa's anti-separatist propaganda efforts, based on the plausible view that they were shallow and more likely to promote than to discourage support for the PQ; and a general desire to appease rather than to provoke the provinces, exemplified by the Clark government's abandonment of lotteries, its promise to transfer jurisdiction over offshore resources to New-foundland, and its politely drawn-out negotiations with Alberta over the price of oil. This approach, like that of the Liberal Party, was the product of the leader's personal instincts rather than of any widespread consideration within the party, either parliamentary or national. Once these points had been made in office, the Clark government gave no further sign of thoughtfulness on the consti-tution. It reduced the temperature of the debate but seemed to have nothing more positive to contribute. Finally, after the govern-ment's defeat in December, Mr Clark made two death-bed offers. He announced, apparently without reflection or consultation, that Senator Arthur Tremblay would lead a federal task force in preparing the government's constitutional proposals (Senator Tremblay, I believe, never received any formal appointment under the Inquiries Act); and he suggested that a new Rowell-Sirois Commission would be necessary to examine the federal-provincial distribution of financial resources, in order to assure the maintenance of sufficient central power—as though the proposed Tremblay study and the question of federal financial distribution were unrelated! This was a disturbingly amateurish way for the prime minister to treat the country's constitutional future; but he and his party apparently had neither the means nor the desire to offer proposals for public discussion more fully considered than Mr Clark's electoral expedients.

The federal NDP, one might have thought, was in an ideal position through the 1970s to play an educative role on constitutional reform. From its founding convention it took a generous position on the French language and the position of Quebec in confederation; at the 1971 convention the party took a compromise stance in favour of constitutional change and even a constituent assembly. The NDP had nothing to lose in Quebec, and perhaps much to gain, by opting for a major alteration in the distribution of powers. It would have fulfilled its national vocation as the spur to reform had it insisted upon and developed those early attitudes in confident public debate. Instead it found them embarrassing and buried them. The party seemed unable to stand up against Mr Trudeau's intimidating scorn of anyone who doubted the righteousness of his federalism, or against the rigid centralism of David Lewis, whether as leader or as ex-leader. The NDP did at least continue to debate the constitutional question at its biennial conventions (on the insistence of a determined and persistent minority), but always came out of those conventions after 1971 with a pale reflection of the Liberal government's policy. And Ed Broadbent's apparent personal indifference to the subject ultimately guaranteed that it would have no place in the party's recent electoral appeals.

We are thus faced, I believe, with two federal opposition parties that have abdicated any serious role in the constitutional debate, and a federal government that is demoralized and intellectually exhausted on the subject. That is not an encouraging prospect, even for those who desire a major transfer of power to the provinces, because it suggests that no one in Ottawa knows how to approach the crisis. The possibilities for panic and imprudent reaction to the pressures of the moment are ominous. There is no indication of any strong commitment in either English-speaking Canada or Quebec to the maintenance of the federal union in its present balance, but rather a striking absence of conviction about the role of the central government. The unusually vacuous nature of the recent federal election campaign, I think, underlines that absence of conviction. On the other hand, what confronts Ottawa's disintegrating defence of the central authority is the powerful mythology of popular sovereignty and nationalism in Quebec, and a new sense of power, enhanced by greed, in Alberta and its neighbouring provinces of the West.

What alone might rally popular support for a renewed assertion of the will and power of the central government (as it has done before) is a widespread perception of national emergency, conceivable in three possible circumstances: an international political crisis threatening world war; an international economic crisis on the scale of the great Depression; or a major crisis of energy supplies. Those circumstances could—and probably would— occur in combination rather than separately; but they are not, I think, events that even the most passionate federalist would wish upon us. Neither are they conditions that Ottawa could easily manufacture in order to justify an assertion of the federal power. Short of this kind of emergency, proclaimed on demonstrable evidence by the federal government and accepted by a strong majority of the population as it probably would be, Ottawa does not appear to possess much psychological leverage in the coming conflict over constitutional power.

Only two political parties, as parties, seem to me to have played a creative role in the evolution of the constitutional debate: the Parti Québécois and the Quebec Liberal Party since the accession of Claude Ryan as its leader. They have both used the party machinery with unusual democratic genius to create and propagate widely their sophisticated programs for constitutional change. The PQ has from the beginning had an instinct about constitutional change in Canada that has proved to be accurate. It takes for granted that Quebec cannot substantially increase its constitutional powers by bargaining from within the established system. This is an instinct about both procedure and substance: that as a province like the others, in federal-provincial conference, Quebec could never gain agreement for its program of constitutional reform; and that even if it could do so in that forum, the alterations gained would not be adequate. In order to reform the system to Quebec's nationalist satisfaction, the Parti Québécois perceives that Quebec must bargain from a position of power outside the normal institutions of federal-provincial diplomacy. The PQ still wishes to bargain, to engage in diplomacy; but it wishes also to reach a satisfactory conclusion to that diplomacy. Twelve years of experience seem to confirm that authoritative decisions cannot be made by the federal-provincial conferences on the constitution; the parties must meet in a new forum, with new leverage. The PQ is well on the way to achieving it.

In Alberta, Saskatchewan, and British Columbia the governments rather than the parties have devoted substantial efforts to the adoption of constitutional programs; and in Ottawa, too, a government, as I have said, once did so after 1968. Elsewhere, including Ontario, I believe that the recent direct contributions of political parties and governments to the debate have been pathetically inadequate. So widespread and profound a failure must point to something more than the political incompetence of all those people and institutions. The forces that make and alter the shapes of nations are, after all, more complex and mysterious than those that make a gasoline tax or a welfare policy, and they are not forces that political parties operating within the rules of the established system can easily perceive or come to terms with. For this reason, that traditional parties elected within an existing constitutional framework cannot in normal times find the focus or the interest to alter that framework, I have sensed for several years that it will require the creation of some extraordinary institutions and procedures to accomplish constitutional reform in Canada: or, alternatively, that change will come about by rupture rather than agreement. One of the problems that will confront Ottawa and the provinces after the Quebec referendum and the next Quebec election—that is, probably, within the next year—will be to consider how to arrange the next and most serious round of constitutional negotiations. The conditioned response will be to return to a series of federal-provincial conferences of first ministers: but those have proven frustrating and futile over the past twelve years because the rule of unanimity has prevented eleven heads of government with differing mandates and interests from reaching general agreement. We will be condemned, I suppose, to more of that before agreement will have to be made to transfer the process to another body, more specifically designed for constitution-making.[4]

For the moment, the Canadian federation lies prostrate and disarmed, the purpose and determination of 1867 drained away, the creative political energies resting with a few provinces of the union who are bursting their constitutional bonds (though not with the same ends in mind). The national government and the national parties, I suspect, have already effectively lost both the battle of Quebec and the battle of the West; it remains to be seen whether the necessary readjustments can be achieved in relative order. But the use of political means to achieve accommodation has not yet been abandoned by anyone, and that is a hopeful sign. The outcome, I am inclined to believe, will not necessarily be a bad thing if life can go on in conditions of liberty, democracy, and common decency in the successor state or states of federal Canada. It is now those conditions, rather than the old federal system, that the parties must apply their talents to preserving.

NOTES

1. Canada. Privy Council Office, *A Future Together: The Task Force on Canadian Unity* (1979), pp. 11-16.
2. George Radwanski, *Trudeau* (Toronto, 1978), pp. 179-80.
3. 'Turning Them Out', *The Canadian Forum*, March 1979.
4. In its claim to negotiate Quebec's status from a position of recognized equality, the Parti Québécois acknowledges the need for a new kind of bargaining process. But aside from suggesting that the other provinces will probably wish to participate with Ottawa on the other side of the bargaining table, and that several negotiating panels might work concurrently, the Quebec White Paper on sovereignty-association leaves the matter vague. The most fully worked-out formula for fresh constitutional discussion appears in the Quebec Liberal Party's document, *A New Canadian Federation*. It proposes the creation of a special constitutional conference, preceded by the adoption of a 'solemn preliminary pledge' to write a new constitution by Parliament and a majority of the provincial legislatures. The conference would have 'a short deadline' of twelve or eighteen months, during which period it would remain in session. The draft constitution produced by the conference would be submitted for ratification to Parliament and the legislatures, and finally to the public in a referendum. The proposal marks a half-step, and perhaps more, toward the concept of a constitutional convention or constituent assembly, and a departure from the ordinary process of federal-provincial diplomacy. This may be a practical, because unobtrusive, means of making that shift.

Robert Craig Brown

FISHWIVES, PLUTOCRATS, SIRENS AND OTHER CURIOUS CREATURES: SOME QUESTIONS ABOUT POLITICAL LEADERSHIP IN CANADA

Perceptions of political leadership are like images in a hall of mirrors. They are partial, shifting, transitory. They often reveal more of the eye and mind of the beholder than of the image reflected. Consider, for example, a recent cartoon which character- ized the leaders of our three national parties as fish-bodied crea- tures with cone-shaped mouths from which emanated pulsing waves of sound. Behind the rock on which they sit, the Canadian voter, in a rowboat, utters a tiny 'Help'.[1] The whole, captioned 'The Sirens', is intended to remind us of Circe's warning to Odys- eus. The Sirens, she admonished, 'bewitch all men'; they 'enchant . . with their clear song . . . and all about them is a great heap of bones of men, corrupt in death'.

Our history is rich with characterizations of our political leaders from the cartoonist's pen, all drawn to accent a momentary image of the leaders' characters or circumstances or both. In 1934 Arch Dale of the *Winnipeg Free Press* placed R.B. Bennett, a portly plutocrat, at the edge of an enormous pile of surplus wheat, the result of R.B.'s high-tariff policy. What, the citizen asked, are we going to do with it? 'Eat it!' Bennett replied.[2] In 1917 Sir Robert Borden, whose government had just passed the Wartime Elections Act, was portrayed as a U-boat captain on the deck of his subma- rine forcing 'Justice', a delicate, scantily clad, and blindfolded beauty, to walk the plank.[3] In 1888 the great cartoonist J.W. Ben- gough drew Sir John A. as an ugly fishwife haggling over a basket of mackerel with Grover Cleveland.[4] At other times Macdonald became a wee lad in tartan short pants, 'Little Johnnie', led by the hand to some dreadful destination or other by John Bull, or a Canadian businessman wearing a vest decorated with dollar signs.

Word portraits by pundits and poets have had the same effect. Recall Dafoe's apt assessment of Laurier as 'a man who had affinities with Machiavelli as well as with Sir Galahad',[5] or A.R.M. Lower on Meighen, 'the lean and hungry Cassius', and Bennett, 'the lord of the iron heel'. When he came to King, Professor Lower found that a pungent phrase would not do. Appropriately, more words were needed to capture the essence of this 'typical', this 'essential' Canadian: 'He spoke as the plain man did—with all the repetitions, the painful elaboration of the obvious, the turgidity of the ordinary man—only more so!'[6] 'We had no shape', Frank Scott wrote of King,

> Because he never took sides,
> And no sides
> Because he never allowed them to take shape.[7]

These images have a lasting appeal. They pinpoint, in their simplicity and directness, contemporary views of leadership, and shape the historical judgement of our political leaders. Even leaders who get scarcely a mention in our texts cannot escape the mirrors of characterization. Because their images are blurred, they neatly fit into the eager student's most frequent class of inquiry: 'Sir J.J.C. who? Sir Mackenzie who?'

There is an elemental truth about these images which we would be foolish to ignore. But, as our friends in political science warn us, we must not stop here. As if to indicate the seriousness of the matter, they have disputed at length the origins and nature of political leadership and constructed a variety of categories in which to put and from which to compare political leaders as diverse as Louis XIV, Gandhi, Charles de Gaulle, and Alexander Mackenzie. Their scholarship goes a long way towards explaining what is and what is not indigenous to political leadership in Canada.

In the typology of leadership political leaders are said to have received their 'legitimization' from any of three sources: God, their own charismatic qualities, or the laws and institutions of the states over which they rule. Numerous musings in Mr King's diary notwithstanding, we can, I think, agree that none of our political leaders received his authority by divine right. (Their pretensions to infallibility are another matter!) On the other hand, journalists and hypesters for the Liberal Party a decade ago tried very hard to convince us that P.E.T. was the very personification of charismatic leadership come to Ottawa. At last we had our own Luther, our own Gandhi, our own Nkrumah, complete with a red Mercedes, with quips for every occasion, and with an adoring cast of thousands of children of all ages. Behind all the flapdoodle, however, was Mr Trudeau the leader we were told that we had been waiting for for so long?

Charismatic leaders are 'transitional figures between old and new forms of authority'—in Charles Taylor's words; 'charisma is like lightning: it is very powerful in short bursts but it does not last very long.' Anyone who listened to Mr Trudeau realized instantly that ushering in a New Order was not his 'thing'; no comment on his longevity seems necessary here. Moreover, charismatic leaders, as an American political scientist puts it, 'believe that they have access to a specific variety of truth' and 'that they have a call to overcome the ignorance and perhaps the evil of those who have not accepted their doctrine.'[8] Again, apart from some Opposition politicians, few of us would agree that Mr Trudeau as party leader and prime minister, whatever else you may think about him, has measured up to this rigid but necessary qualification for charismatic leadership. No, all that happened was that journalists and Liberal propagandists confused a colourful personality with charisma. And, given the rarity of colourful personalities among our political leaders, they may be forgiven their confusion, if not the shallowness of their analysis of Mr Trudeau's character. Roger Graham, in a brilliant essay written shortly after Mr Trudeau came to power, punctured the balloon of charismatic leadership in Canada with a witty question: 'Sir Wilfrid Laurier, let us say, sliding down a banister? Sir Robert Borden in goggles and flippers? Arthur Meighen in a Mercedes? Mackenzie King at judo? R.B. Bennett on skis?'[9]

We are left, as we should be, with our leaders deriving their authority from laws, institutions, and customs that are the fabric of our 'liberal-conservative democratic tradition'. They are selected by political parties operating with formal rules and accepted procedures. They carry out their functions in long-established institutions, like the cabinet and Parliament. A closer look at this process will reveal some of the boundaries and some of the opportunities of Canadian political leadership.

William Lyon Mackenzie King in 1919, and Richard Bedford Bennett almost a decade later, were the first national party leaders elected by party leadership conventions. Earlier leaders had been selected by the party hierarchy or by the party caucus. Borden's selection in 1901 illustrated the latter case; he was elected from among contenders in the caucus with the open support of the retiring leader, Sir Charles Tupper. Arthur Meighen was the last party leader to be chosen by caucus and the mode of his selection was probably unique. The Unionist caucus cast preferential ballots for their new leader. But the caucus also specified that the ballots were advisory and explicitly delegated to Borden the unwelcome task of selecting his own successor and persuading his colleagues to support Meighen.[10]

Even in these extraordinary circumstances, a primary criterion for selection as leader was a broad measure of demonstrated support in the ranks of the caucus, or, after 1919, in the party's convention. Borden and King, and probably Laurier and Macdonald, among others, were elected because, to borrow Frank Underhill's phrase, they were leaders 'who divided us least'. They were leaders who had been loyal party men, men who recognized that they were creatures of their parties. 'I am their leader, I must follow them,' quotes Léon Dion: 'the leader's role as innovator will be accepted only after he has given proof of his absolute loyalty to the group.'[11]

No one demonstrated this axiom of interdependence between the leader and his party more deliberately or more expertly than Mr King. He might outrage functionaries in the National Liberal Federation[12] and he might cow his colleagues into submission to his will with a pointed reminder of *his* role as leader, as he did during the 1944 conscription crisis when he told the cabinet that 'as the leader of the Party ... I had to consider what was owing to the Party.'[13] Nevertheless, as Blair Neatby observes, the caucus was King's 'sounding board' and 'his test for any measure was its effect on party unity or national unity.' Because King believed the Liberal Party was the 'political embodiment' of the diverse interests and regions of the nation, party unity and national unity were usually synonymous.[14]

Interdependence required that prime ministers should have, as Lord Dufferin said of Macdonald, a 'great faculty for managing other people'. Macdonald's problems with 'loose fish' never ceased. 'It has kept me constantly at work to the exclusion of everything else,' he wrote in 1881, 'to strengthen the weak-hearted in both Houses.' 'Loose fish' were less a problem for Macdonald's successors as party discipline stiffened and the institution of the caucus became formalized. Even so, the papers of every prime minister are filled with comments echoing Sir John A.'s. Every party, every caucus, and every cabinet has had its quota of 'weak-hearted' and the not-always-gentle art of persuasion remains an essential attribute of a party leader.

The nature of the national parties, with some exception granted for the Co-operative Commonwealth Federation and the New Democratic Party, also discouraged dramatic policy initiatives by party leaders. The problem was twofold: not to alienate the support the leader enjoyed and to acquire new adherents to the party. The aim of a party's spokesman, Borden argued, was to 'seek to reach and influence men of moderate opinion who vote now with one and now with the other party.'[16] The prescription for success was a restrained approach to partisanship and a wary attitude towards innovation. Sir John A., Creighton observed, 'was not a crusader with a mission'; 'he thumped no tubs and banged no pulpits.'[17] Similarly, Laurier, as Skelton put it, 'was never a man to raise questions before they were ripe'.[18] And King, the master of the 'half measure', 'saw no need for political action when political harmony did not seem threatened.'[19]

At first sight we have a paradox here. The party leader as manager, as persuader, as 'Old Tomorrow', as the artisan of half-measures, projects an image of pandering to debilitating but necessary compromise. But Charles Taylor reminds us, albeit disapprovingly, that national parties that aim at this kind of broad support must, of necessity, emphasize their capacity for leadership. Eschewing specific program promises, they offer electors 'a leadership which claims the competence to extract and act on the consensus at any given time, rather than a specific view of what should be done.'[20]

'Reforms are for Oppositions,' Laurier once remarked. 'It is the business of governments to stay in office.'[21] Put another way, the business of government is power, and the power of the prime minister to do something—and to do nothing—is most evident in the cabinet. Here too a complex relationship between the government leader, his party, his caucus, and his cabinet colleagues is constantly at work, creating opportunities for and imposing limitations on his leadership.

Macdonald, who described himself as a 'cabinetmaker', told a friend that 'a good carpenter . . . can work with indifferent tools.'[22] He was referring, confidently, to his ability to get the best out of indifferent cabinet colleagues. But there was a limit. Both he and Laurier began their administrations with cabinets composed of able and powerful men. Both had to rely on men of lesser talents as time went on, and their own power and prestige slipped accordingly. Borden began with a relatively weak cabinet; the infusion of new blood in 1917 freed him to implement a creative initiative in external affairs and gave his Union government the power and prestige that were not evident in his first administration. Clearly, a powerful and talented colleague like C.D. Howe,[23] given the freedom to pursue innovative policies, contributed to the impression of strong leadership by Mackenzie King. Indeed, Samuel Tilley's National Policy and Clifford Sifton's immigration policy, to cite two examples, became hallmarks of the Macdonald and Laurier governments.

⨯Each prime minister, of course, had his own style of cabinet leadership. Laurier often conveyed an impression of aloofness from the business of government and liked to say, 'I'm a lazy dog.'[24] But his ears were always up. 'A masterful man set on having his own way,' Sifton remarked; 'and equally resolute that his colleagues shall not have their way unless this is quite agreeable to him.'[25] Borden generally presided over his cabinet as a genial committee chairman. King, Mr Pearson observed, 'was the headmaster!'—adding that 'my philosophy was to let a Cabinet Minister, as far as possible, run his own show and that it was not my job to be interfering in details.'[26] Most prime ministers worked hard to avoid divisions in their cabinets, but when difficult and divisive decisions had to be made, as Mr Diefenbaker said, 'the final responsibility rests on the Prime Minister. No one else.'[27] The prime minister, if he wished, could also assume initial responsibility for some policy and ignore his cabinet colleagues. But the historical record suggests that this has been a game full of risks. Laurier's schools policy for the new provinces, Bennett's 'New Deal', Pearson's compromise with Quebec on the pension plan, and, in some respects, Borden's conscription policy, remind us of leaders in trouble rather than in control.

The price for such daring and sometimes desperate gambles is usually paid in the House of Commons. Political scientists differ sharply on the role the House of Commons plays in an evaluation of political leadership. Thomas Hockin reminds us that the rules and procedures of the House are designed to favour the Opposition and that the prime minister, who can speak as the leader of the nation outside the House, is forced to play the part of partisan chieftain in that 'theatre for political upheavals'.[28] But, Denis Smith replies, 'in its less spectacular day-to-day performances, the House of Commons normally, if grudgingly, does the work the Government directs it to do.'[29]

The first article in every prime minister's profession of faith must be, as Pearson put it, 'a deep and genuine feeling for Parliamentary institutions.' That does not mean that they all liked their work there. 'I never had any great love of Parliamentary battles and rows,' Pearson said. 'I used to get impatient because you couldn't get things done quickly enough because of those struggles in Parliament that other people may have loved.'[30] St Laurent, King, and Borden would have agreed. And recalling that Diefenbaker, Drew, Meighen, and Laurier sat across the aisle, the sentiment is understandable. Other prime ministers obviously enjoyed the place: Diefenbaker for its theatrical potential; Laurier as an arena for his eloquence; Macdonald as a partisan battleground and as the most congenial club in Canada.

This suggests a necessary change of focus in our examination of political leadership. So far I have concentrated upon the role that the political institutions of our society play in restraining or encouraging displays of leadership. I have been using, and no doubt abusing, what political scientists call a 'situational' mode of evaluation and it does yield essential insight into the nature of leadership in a democratic society. There is, however, a whiff of stasis and determinism in all this. It is already apparent in the examples I have cited that institutional limits and opportunities are only one factor in our inquiry.

As Donald Creighton observed, every historical study is an 'encounter between character and circumstances'.[31] Both beg far more questions than can be answered, or even acknowledged here. But a few examples of the influence of circumstances and character on the decisions of our political leaders are in order.

Circumstances, political deadlock in the Canadas, indecisive tinkering with the idea of union in the Maritimes, civil war in the United States, and growing problems in Anglo-American relations, among many factors, provided the opportunity and shaped the nature of Confederation, Macdonald's—and George Brown's—greatest political achievement. And circumstances, the unforeseen growth of provincial powers and responsibilities, dramatically altered the nature of Confederation before Macdonald's death. Circumstances, a decade of prosperity, low interest rates, expanding export markets for Canadian natural products, cheap shipping fares, industrial innovation and expansion in Canada, and a shrewd sense of timing, made the Laurier government's immigration policy a success. That, in turn, made the creation of the new provinces necessary and politically opportune. Moreover, circumstances, the legacies of earlier school crises and the dwindling influence of the francophone minority in the Territories, influenced the nature of Laurier's original schools clauses in the Autonomy Bills *and* the opposition to them in his own ranks and in the Opposition party. Circumstances played a major role in Borden's decision to abandon his pledge that there would be no conscription in World War I. Conscription, another circumstance, helped King to win the Liberal Party leadership and a long series of elections. It also deeply influenced his tenacious resistance to conscription in World War II and his eventual half-abandonment of voluntary enlistment.

But remember that at every moment in a political leader's career there is an interplay, an 'encounter', between circumstances and character. His own perception of the restraints and the opportunities of institutions and of circumstances is also shaped by his own personality. In the end, I think, this is the most important determinant in what he does, in what he refuses to do, in the quality and the success or failure of his leadership.

Leaving aside the pretensions Mr King confided to his diary, none of our political leaders had been born to rule. But wanting to rule and having extraordinary confidence in their capacity and fitness to rule are characteristics that set our memorable political leaders apart from other men. Compare, for example, the responses of Mr Diefenbaker and Sir Mackenzie Bowell to the cabinet revolts each endured. 'The Chief' faced his down; Bowell succumbed. Poor Sir Mackenzie, unlike Diefenbaker, seems not to have wanted to fight for his leadership. As Laurier said of Alexander Mackenzie, 'he has no zest to carry a party on.' Mackenzie admitted as much. 'From the first,' he said while prime minister, 'I was more willing to serve than reign.'[32] And yet another prime minister, Sir John Joseph Caldwell Abbott, began his term of office with what amounted to an apology: 'I am here very much because I am not particularly obnoxious to anybody.'[33] A redeeming quality, no doubt, and one that was true of many other Canadian political leaders. But Abbott was not 'here' long—five months and eight days. The lack of 'zest' for leadership, then, is a sure first step to oblivion.

But listen to Laurier's reaction to his first election to the Quebec legislature: 'I have scored a triumph, a real triumph.' His goal, he said, was 'making my ideas triumph,' surely the most ambitious of all political goals.[34] His confidence occasionally wavered but never died. Towards the end of his long career, early in the 1917 conscription crisis, Laurier told a friend that 'if at the present time anybody can restrain and face the extremists, I think I am the man.'[35]

King shared Laurier's confidence and his will to triumph, but not his 'zest'. Here is King on his last electoral victory:

It was almost as if I had had a bath after a dusty and dirty journey, with the storm of lies, misrepresentations, insinuations and what in which I have had to pass during the past few weeks—I might even say over most of the years of the war. One could go back and say almost over one's public life. I felt a real vindication in the verdict of the people and a sense of triumph therefrom.[36]

That speaks volumes about King's perception of his leadership and reminds us of the striking differences that accompanied the similarities in the personalities of two of our most successful political leaders.[37]

Courage, determination, patience, tolerance, all in varying measure, are also characteristics of nearly all our political leaders. Each of us can supply his own examples. I think of Macdonald, who had all these qualities. Macdonald, however, seemed to find his way through encounters with circumstances with an especial flair. A less demanding and inquiring, or prying, age, of course, allowed more assistance from the grape and the grain and Macdonald took full advantage of that. But Macdonald bore his defeats and dreadful tragedy in his private life with uncommon cheer and wit and a healthy pinch of fatalism. 'Take things pleasantly,' he told a friend, 'and when fortune empties her chamber pot on your head—smile and say, "we are going to have a summer shower." ' [38]

One final example of how personality encounters and moulds circumstances. Compare, for a moment, the approaches of Borden and King to conscription in 1917 and 1944. There are, in fact, remarkable similarities in the circumstances leading to each crisis, but the motivations of the two men were as different as day and night. Borden's decision was rooted in his complete commitment to the soldiers, a commitment steeled by his hours of visits with wounded men during his trips to England and France in 1915 and 1917. Borden had made a covenant with 'his boys'. 'No man wanting inspiration, determination or courage as to his duty in this war ... could go to any better place than the hospitals in which our Canadian boys are to be found,' he said on the day he announced his decision for conscription. 'I should feel myself unworthy ... if I did not fulfill my pledge.' [39]

Mr King was no less concerned about the welfare of the Canadian troops in World War II, but his concern was more abstract; the emotional fervour that drove Borden was absent. And King was torn, far more than Borden, between the demands of the military and his fear of national disunity and internal strife. In the end King rationalized his turnabout with two imagined conspiracies by opponents of his social reforms and by plotters in the army. 'King', Professor Granatstein remarks, 'had to create these dark shadows before he could bring himself to take drastic and difficult action.' [40]

Our perceptions of political leadership are shaped by a host of images. We probably judge yesterday's fishwives more justly than we do today's Sirens, if only because time adds evidence, balance,

and perspective. Our political institutions, our history and contemporary circumstances, create restraints upon and offer opportunities for initiative and innovation by our political leaders. But
institutions, history, and circumstances are their chamber pots of
fortune. How did they, with their complex and unique personalities, respond when the chamber pots tipped? That is the most
important question in our inquiry. Did they smile—or curse the
gods?

NOTES

1. *The Globe and Mail*, 2 January 1980, p. 6.
2. J.M.S. Careless and R. Craig Brown, eds, *The Canadians, 1867-1961* (Toronto, 1967), p. 245.
3. *Regina Morning Leader*, 13 September 1917, p. 1.
4. Robert Craig Brown, *Canada's National Policy, 1883-1900* (Princeton, 1964), p. 87.
5. John Dafoe, *Laurier: A Study in Canadian Politics* (Toronto, 1922), p. 15.
6. Cited in J.M. Beck and D.J. Dooley, 'Party Images in Canada', in Hugh A. Thorburn, ed., *Party Politics in Canada* (Toronto, 1963), pp. 33, 37.
7. 'W.L.M.K.', in F.R. Scott and A.J.M. Smith, eds, *The Blasted Pine* (Toronto, 1957), p. 27.
8. Charles Taylor, 'Political Leadership and Polarization in Canadian Politics', in Thomas A. Hockin, ed., *Apex of Power: The Prime Minister and Political Lead-ership in Canada* (Scarborough, 1971), p. 112; Robert S. Robins, 'Paranoia and Charisma', unpublished paper.
9. Roger Graham, 'Charisma and Canadian Politics', in John S. Moir, ed., *Charac-ter and Circumstance: Essays in Honour of Donald Grant Creighton* (Toronto, 1970), p. 26.
10. Robert Craig Brown, *Robert Laird Borden: A Biography*, vol. 1 (Toronto, 1975), ch. 3; vol. 2 (Toronto, 1980), ch. 14.
11. Léon Dion, 'The Concept of Political Leadership: An Analysis', *Canadian Journal of Political Science*, 1 (March 1968), p. 4.
12. See Reginald Whitaker, *The Government Party: Organizing and Financing the Liberal Party of Canada, 1930-58* (Toronto, 1977), passim.
13. Cited in J.L. Granatstein, *Canada's War: The Politics of the Mackenzie King Government, 1939-1945* (Toronto, 1978), p. 347.
14. H. Blair Neatby, *William Lyon Mackenzie King, vol. 3, 1932-39* (Toronto, 1976), pp. 4-14.
15. Donald Creighton, *John A. Macdonald: The Old Chieftain* (Toronto, 1957), pp. 251, 309.
16. Henry Borden, ed., *Letters to Limbo* (Toronto, 1971), pp. 68-9.
17. Donald Creighton, *John A. Macdonald: The Young Politician* (Toronto, 1952), p. 180.

18. O.D. Skelton, *The Life and Letters of Sir Wilfrid Laurier*, vol. 1 (Garden City, 1922), p. 362.

19. Neatby, *King*, vol. 3, pp. 11-13.

20. Taylor, 'Political Leadership', p. 110.

21. Cited in Paul Stevens, 'Wilfrid Laurier: Politician', in Marcel Hamelin, ed., *Les Idées politiques des Premiers Ministres canadiens* (Ottawa, 1969), p. 14.

22. Cited in P.B. Waite, 'The Political Ideas of John A. Macdonald', in Hamelin, *Les Idées politiques*, p. 54.

23. See Robert Bothwell and William Kilbourn, *C.D. Howe: A Biography* (Toronto, 1979).

24. Skelton, *Laurier*, vol. 2, p. 163.

25. Cited in Stevens, 'Laurier', p. 73.

26. 'Interview with the Right Honourable Lester B. Pearson', in Hockin, *Apex of Power*, p. 197.

27. 'Interview with the Right Honourable John G. Diefenbaker', in Hockin, *Apex of Power*, p. 185.

28. 'The Prime Minister and Political Leadership: An Introduction to Some Restraints and Imperatives', in Hockin, *Apex of Power*, pp. 7-10.

29. Denis Smith, 'President and Parliament: The Transformation of Parliamentary Government in Canada', in Hockin, *Apex of Power*, p. 234.

30. 'Interview with Pearson', in Hockin, *Apex of Power*, p. 194.

31. Donald Creighton, *Towards the Discovery of Canada* (Toronto, 1972), p. 19.

32. Skelton, *Laurier*, vol. 1, pp. 187, 181.

33. *Ibid.*, p. 430.

34. *Ibid.*, pp. 110-11.

35. Brown, *Borden*, vol. 2.

36. Cited in Granatstein, *Canada's War*, p. 410.

37. Laurier saved his darker reflections for electoral defeats. 'It is becoming more and more manifest to me', he wrote in October 1911, 'that it was not reciprocity that was turned down, but a Catholic premier.'

38. Cited in Waite, 'The Political Ideas of John A. Macdonald', p. 66.

39. Canada, Parliament, House of Commons, *Debates*, 18 May 1917, pp. 1539, 1542.

40. Granatstein, *Canada's War*, p. 423.